Still Brai... & Co...g

By Laura Roodman-Edwards-Ray

(Pick a name, any name)

Copyright © 2013 Laura Edwards Ray
ISBN: 978-1-891442-85-8

Editor: Fran Levy
Cover illustration by Rachel Pursley
Laura's photo by The Snappin Sistas
Judy Coday-Nancy Lister- Angie Gellner
Bluebird Publishing Co.
St. Louis, MO
www.BluebirdBookPub.com

Acknowledgements

Once again, if I didn't have friends and family that loved me and put up with all of my drama, this book would never have come to fruition.

I am eternally grateful to Team Roodman who are food photographers extraordinaire. Thank you Jason, JoJo, and David for all of their tireless work making sure that all of the recipes I've cooked look their best. And many thanks to Carol for always cleaning up her kitchen with a smile after I've totally destroyed it.

To my Mother- thank you for always supporting me and being my biggest fan.

To Barb, Wendy, and David – You are not only my sisters and brother, but you've always been the best friends anyone could ever have. Your continual love and support always amazes me. I'm not exaggerating when I say that I would never have survived had it not been for all three of you.

To my kids, thank you for your unconditional love and allowing me the time to continue to have a blast while I'm fulfilling this dream of mine.

And finally to Tom, you will always be the love of my life and I hope I didn't embarrass you too much this time.

I dedicate this book to every person out there who is currently or has been in an abusive relationship. I hope you are able to get out of it and thrive.

Table of Contents

Chapter 25
A Simple Way to Piss Off a Total Stranger

Chapter 26
I Continually Tell Myself How Truly Blessed I Am

Chapter 1

The Aftermath

Well, all I have to say is that I absolutely loved writing my first book. I know that we all have our own "stories," but I felt like it was an absolute privilege to write mine out and have other people read it. It actually beats the hell of every therapy session I've ever had, and believe me, I've been through a few of them.

In fact, I'd recommend it to all of my new BFFs. It's been a "bucket list" type of thing, and now that I've done it, it's a little addictive. So, as I've said before, when I finally have the pleasure to meet you, I will feel compelled to give you the $20 co-pay. Or better yet, how about a margarita and an appetizer (much more fun than $20, which if you're like me, would just go toward paying the damn water bill or something equally boring).

So, the book came out and I don't know what I expected. I knew that Oprah wasn't going to be calling me anytime soon. It wasn't her fault – her show was ending. If "retiring" means starting an entire television network, and that is why she didn't have time to read my book and call me. That's OK. Hopefully someone in her entourage will find the time to pick up one of my books and fall in love with it. Laura Ray has a dream!

I have realized (and have been told on numerous occasions) that my books are perfect for anyone who has any kind of Attention Deficit Disorder. It's really a good thing, because I think, "we," as Women of the Millennium (and the few men who "got it"), who have to be multitaskers extraordinaire, would really be in deep doo doo if we didn't have some degree of ADD. Hell, without it, I don't think we'd ever be able to find the time to pee, so thank goodness for that!

I also was in my "La La Land" believing that everyone would think I was as funny as I thought I was. I always laugh at my own jokes and I'm always quite perplexed when people just look at me as though I've totally lost it. Well, I was pleasantly surprised that most people did "get it." I've been blessed many times to have spoken at book clubs where they have featured my book (usually, where the women bring their favorite recipes from the book, or will pick their favorite chapter and choose the recipe that goes with it), and they have been a genuine honor as well as a "hoot."

We basically start out with talking about what "number" each person is – the informative takeaway from my silly numerology chapter, or talk about whether any of the readers have ever divorced a friend (or were the divorcees—which of course is just as painful!). And then we all talk about how many of those in the group have my "disease", GT (aka: Generosity Tourettes.) It's amazing how many of us have it. So many that I think you will be able to find a "GT Anonymous" group near you in the very near future.

But, with all of the sweet things that have been said about the book, there have been just as many people who knock you down to size. This is a very good thing, and hopefully with all of the constructive criticism I've received, it will just make this book and those that follow better and easier to stomach.

One of those constructive critics happened to be my brother Johnny's mother-in-law. (Johnny also doubles as my best friend and food photographer, even though photography isn't even close to his "real" profession.) What she said was so hilarious and so dead on, that I knew immediately that I would have to put it in the first chapter of my second book.

I was at a family birthday party when this sweet, very religious, super-über-to-the-right conservative (my husband Sven and she get along quite well...NOT!) came up to me and, as God is my witness, said, "Lou, I just want to tell you something." I said, "Oh, Grandma Betty (yes, she's the infamous Grandma Betty of the Grandma Betty's Heath Bar Cake recipe.) Though when I made it on a local news show to promote the book, she said, "Oh my, you sure do use a lot more caramel, chocolate chips and butter than I ever did." (Go figure). Anyway, she continued, "I just finished reading your book and I have to tell you, I was a bit taken aback by it." Here I was with my Sharpie, ready to sign her book, and I thought, "Oh shit, here it comes." She said, "I have to tell you, I was upset that you used way too many swear words throughout the entire book, you said the word 'orgasm' five times (to think that she counted is pretty cool in itself, don't you think?), and honestly Lou," here comes the part that just cracked me up—in a nervous, kind of eye-twitchy type of way) "*I learned more about you than I ever wanted to know!*"

It kind of hit me like a ton of bricks when she said that. Here I was— writing to my new best friends. But it ended up being mostly people I had never met, thinking that they would hopefully relate to some of the things I've lived through. (I can't be the only person out there who has made so many stupid mistakes, can I?)

And then it hit me: I just told this 77-year-old Republican woman about my failed marriage(s), goofy children, 16-pound Chihuahua and, of course, my orgasms.

What the hell was I thinking?

Next, there was my fabulous, semi-celebrity husband. Please let me preface this by saying that I began this little hobby when I couldn't sleep one early morning. He was snoring sweetly next to me and the girls were at a slumber party. So, I went down to the basement and typed up a few chapters (I think my first one was the "cow pie" story), and when I was done, I went back upstairs, woke him up and asked him very politely to read them.

He wasn't upset at all. My sweet Sven just looked at me, and said, "Honey, I didn't know you like to write." Then he sweetly propped himself up with about six pillows, and within about 27 seconds he began to actually laugh out loud. Sven is way more subdued than *moi*, and when I saw him laughing, even in his semi-awake state, I knew that I had done something right. I felt a HUGE sense of accomplishment. (It doesn't take much!)

When I finally got the book together to have it published, I gave the entire thing to him and, in the kindest words that I could muster (deep down I was nervous as hell), I said, "Honey, please read this – and if you find anything that I've written embarrassing to you at all, just tell me and I'll take it out. (I thought, "Shit, this is my third marriage only of course, if you count P.D. twice. Thank God Sven doesn't. He always says 'one penis counts for one marriage.' God, I *love* how he does math! and I don't want to blow our wonderful marriage with my goofy memoir. That would be really stupid and counter-productive, don't you think?

Well, my husband had the book on his computer at work for 6 months and *never* looked at it. I guess he assumed that everything would be fine.

I'll never forget the day the book came out: November 22, 2010, to be exact. My loving husband looked at me and said, "I can't believe you wrote about &%& and *&^%. He then looked at me and said, "Honey, I love you – but Sweetie, *what the hell were you thinking?!*" He continued, "I even just ordered a t-shirt that I'm going to start wearing, called *"Confessions of a Man Named Sven."*

I looked at him and said, "Honey, man that I love, you had 6 damn months to read what I wrote. I guess you didn't read any of it in the *6 months that you had to proofread it,* did you, Dear?" I then said, "I bet when I finish my next book, you'll definitely read through it, won't you?"

He looked at the ground and very sheepishly said, "I think I'll just hire a team of proofreaders and make sure that you don't say anything more about our private lives!" What is that old saying, "If you snooze – you lose"?

One of the nicest letters I received, a few weeks after the book came out, was from one of Sven's good friends's girlfriend, who I had never met. Sven's friend, Frankie, came over to the house to help fix up our kitchen after the pipe broke and the entire kitchen had to be re-done. He worked for a few weeks until late at night on it after his "day job," and he did such a great job. Since he spent many nights at our home instead of with his girlfriend (because of our entire family's inability to do any handiwork around the house at all) besides paying him, I decided to give him a copy of my new book to give to her. A few weeks later, I received this lovely thank-you letter:

Dear Laura,

Thank you so much for sharing your book with me. I so enjoyed reading it!

I started it the Thursday or Friday that Frankie brought it home to me and was finished by the end if the weekend! I honestly look forward to reading the next volume!

When Frankie, a while ago, brought home a tray of dessert — minus a few small servings, I was flabbergasted! I couldn't understand why you would go through all that work to make a dessert for your family and then send it all with Frankie?

Well, now I know why. It is just who you are and I have enjoyed getting to know you!

Thank you again for all of your kindness and thoughtfulness! Linda

The funniest thing about this letter to me was that I couldn't believe that either I, the girls or Sven actually took a few brownies and blueberry bars off the dessert tray before we gave it to Frankie to give to her. What tacky pigs we are! It was the sweetest letter, but it cracked me up.

The last story I'll bore you with is about my big sister Babs. I was really worried about the chapter I wrote about her. I actually lost sleep about the chapter about when she signed me up for that lovely, nationally syndicated show, "What Not to Wear." I do want you all to know that before the book had its final proofread, I said, "Babs, did you read the chapter I wrote about you? You have to tell me the truth, and if I've hurt your feelings at all, I'll take the chapter out."

I continued to ramble on, "you know that I love you more than anything and hurting your feelings would kill me, and of course, that wasn't my intention at all!"

Do you know what my wonderful sister, who I love more than life itself, said? She said (verbatim; you must know that I couldn't make this stuff up even if I tried!), "Oh no, Lou, you didn't hurt my feelings at all." "In fact, your book is so good, that I think you'll be famous one day! So what I'm going to do is to call back the people at the show right away and tell them that they have to hurry up and help you immediately! This book of yours may just make you famous and you're really going to need all the help they can give you as soon as possible!"

The moral of this chapter is that I always needlessly end up worrying about the dumbest things.

This is one of my favorite "comfort foods" of all times, especially when I'm feeling a wee bit anxious and neurotic.

LOU'S "IN THE NEWS" SHRIMP CHEESY GRITS

1 lb of large shrimp, peeled and deveined
1 sliced red pepper
1 sliced yellow pepper
1/2 cup of chopped red onions
1 lb of cooked chicken sausage
1/2 tsp of minced garlic
salt and pepper to taste
1/2 cup white wine
1/2 cup of grape tomatoes

In a large skillet, sauté the red peppers, yellow peppers, red onions, chicken sausage, garlic, salt and pepper in 2 tbsp of unsalted butter and ¼ cup of olive oil.
Add wine and tomatoes.
Add shrimp and cook for 3 to 5 minutes, until shrimp turns pink.
Add 1 tbsp chopped parsley

Cheesy Grits

Bring 1 cup of water and 1/2 tsp salt to a boil

Add 3 cups of milk and 1 cup of quick-cooking grits (If you're making more, make sure that your ratio of grits to liquid is 4:1) and bring to a boil.
Reduce heat, add 1 cup of Gouda cheese, 1 cup of shredded cheddar cheese, add 1 tbsp unsalted butter.
Stir constantly until thick and well blended.
Serve on a plate: heap the shrimp mixture on top of the grits.

Enjoy. I hope you like this one as much I do!

Chapter 2

The Four Questions

I'm sure that my Jewish readers (and many of the non-Jewish readers, for that matter!) know of the four questions that the youngest child must read during the traditional Passover seder service. They are significant not only because of their meaning, but also because recitation of the four questions means that soon – finally! – we get to eat the delicious, elaborate meal. Don't worry; the four questions that I'm referring to in this chapter are not those.

I'm actually referring to the four questions that I've been asked most frequently since my first memoir came out. As I've said before, my writing style is very similar to the way I talk—which, as I've said before, is why my books are perfect for anyone with any kind of Attention Deficit Disorder. I'm sure that you've realized that you can really skip around anywhere in my books and you won't be lost (unlike the author, of course!). But, by the questions I've been asked, I realized that I needed to clarify some things that confused readers.

Please let me explain. You see, in my teeny tiny little mind, even though I had never met you before, I had already made you my new best friend. I told you all of my deepest, darkest, most embarrassing stories. I guess I just assumed you would understand why I did some of the things that I did. So, when I realized that a lot of readers actually had never met me, I understood why these totally sane and rational human beings couldn't understand some of my behavior. That is why I thought that it might be smart to use this chapter to answer the four questions that I have been asked constantly since the book came out last year.

Question 1. Why the hell did you ever marry Psycho Dick for the second time?

Answer: I guess the reason why I didn't spell it out, is that I wanted to make the book an easy, funny and enjoyable read that most everyone would relate to. Everybody has stories, and I promise that once you write yours, I'll read it. Writing has been such a therapeutic endeavor that, as I've said before, I feel like I owe every single person who has ever read my book a $20 co-pay. (Once you finish this one, you may submit your voucher for another $20!). But, even though I told you most everything, I have two beautiful, teenage daughters to worry about. Oh, and we must not forget about P.D., who lives about 12 miles away from us. Needless to say, I was a wee bit worried about his reaction to the chapters I wrote about our two marriages. Oh well, Karma is a quite the bitch, don't you think? You know what? I'd love for him to write his own book to tell his story. My wonderful Sven has always said that I was way too kind when writing about my first-second husband.

Anyway, to answer the question as to why I took him back after he morphed into full-fledged P.D., all I can say is that spousal abuse is an insidious thing. I was told day in and day out that I was stupid and fat, that no one would ever give me a second look because of my big, cellulite butt, that I was lucky to have him, and that deep down I really wanted to screw my brother. (I never understood that one, because *he* was the one who was originally from Arkansas.). After 7 years of that, I truly believed that everything he said probably had a ring of truth to it. It got to the point that I just wanted him to have an affair with some skanky woman he met at one of the bars he hung out at all the time, or hit me once (just lightly, I'm only a semi-masochist), because I thought that would give me the perfect excuse to "Run… Forrest Run."

Of course, he never did that – that would be way too easy, and I was his handy dandy meal ticket and total schmuck. Instead, he methodically berated me and made me feel like this would be the best it would ever be. Oh, and of course that he wouldn't be able to survive if I left him.

When I left the first time, I was 34 years old and we didn't have kids. Perfect, right? No strings attached, easy to run, start a new life. WRONG! That was actually worse for me, because at that point I didn't care about myself at all. His kids—who I helped raise the best I could for years— and his lovely parents (I'll talk about them in another chapter, and definitely will have an alcoholic beverage with a nice little umbrella as the recipe for that chapter to calm all of our nerves) called to tell me that P.D. was totally devastated, and had "holed" himself up in the little cabin that we owned 2 hours away. They told me that if I didn't take him back and give him someplace to stay, they knew that he would probably harm himself (can you read between these lines?).

I was scared to death. He was the first man that I really ever loved, and I truly was stupid enough to think that I could "save" this asshole. I called him and told him that we could work out our problems if he would

1. Go to A.A. and get help

2. Change and become Dick White again. the real Dick who I had loved so much and who I knew was "in there" somewhere…NOT!

He immediately did not "pass go or collect $200." He jumped into his car and drove back to suburbiaville, and about 2 weeks later, I found out that I was pregnant with Maggie. Co-dependency and trying to change the world is a scary ass thing.

But who cares? I was thrilled beyond my imagination. I thought that this was God's way of telling me that I was doing the right thing. I wanted to be a mommy so badly. Anyway, of course God forbid I have a child out of wedlock, so we got married again (we actually waited for our old anniversary date to get re-married. That way, P.D. didn't have to remember 2 dates for our anniversary. Isn't that just pathetic? I was trying to be kind to a pickled mind mind. I think that could be a song, what do you think?)

When Maggie was born, I was in such baby-la-la-land heaven that I pretended that everything was fine. The reality was that he hid liquor all over the house and woke up smashed on his ass on Sunday mornings. But then again, he kept telling me that it was just a "chemical imbalance" and I was stupid to think that he was drinking in a home that had no alcohol. He would constantly say, "You dumb bitch, I'm sober as a judge…sober as a judge!"

I think that subliminally I didn't want Maggie to be an only child; and even though I'm sure that I knew that I wouldn't be in this hell forever, I got pregnant again right away with Mollie. I think I knew that I would end up raising them by myself, and that was good enough for me. My two wonderful children and I would prevail and live happily ever after.

I actually tell the girls at least once a week that they are the reason I'm alive today and the reason why I finally left him. I'm sure that I'm not alone with this one. I'll try to explain. You see, once I had my girls, I knew that I could not care less about his happiness and welfare. He was not my priority anymore. My main priority was to be the best mom I could possibly be with these two beautiful babies that I'd brought into this world. And I'd be damned if they were going to be raised in a home where any type of abuse occurred.

So anyway, I guess, long story short, the reason why I divorced him the first time was because I shouldn't have ever married him in the first place; and the reason why I married and divorced him the second time was because of the two best things that ever happened to me—Maggie and Mollie.

Question 2. *Where on Earth is South Bumble%&$*?*

Answer: I feel guilty about this one, so I'm going to keep it a secret even from my new BFF's!

When I did my first book signing, someone asked me where it was and I told her the truth. She glared at me as if I had punched her 98-year-old grandmother in the stomach, and said, "Well, you might hate South Bumble%$*&, but I absolutely love it and I can't believe you said the things about it that you did!." So, please let me say, I never ever wanted to hurt anyone's feelings. About 98.967 percent of my books are about me, making fun of the stupid things that I have done in the past. And it's really just the opinion of a very naïve, young and stupid woman who was a total fish out of water in a small, gossip-ridden town where they thought Jews had horns—that's all!

Question 3. *Is Sven's name really Sven?*

Answer: No, I just made it up and he absolutely hates it! He said that he sounds like a gay masseuse! He actually had two t-shirts made: one that says "Don't Call Me Sven!" and another that says, "Confessions from a man named Sven!" I think Sven sounds like a gorgeous, blonde Swedish guy who sits by the fire in a gorgeous ski resort with a very cool turtleneck sweater, whispering sweet nothings in my ear holding my coffee with a hint of Bailey's Irish Cream. In reality, my wonderful husband is the exact opposite of that. Not only would he never step foot in a ski resort, he rarely wears sweaters. You may just meet him one day and wonder what the hell I was thinking when I named him "Sven." The truth is, he's *my* "Sven," I love him madly, and I was trying to keep him anonymous.

OH WELL — TOO LATE

Question 4. How did you ever meet Sven?

Answer: This one is quite the funny story, and a little embarrassing. I won't go into all the details, but as I said in my first book, one of my best friends thought that the reason why I had such horrible luck in marriage was the fact that P.D. is not Jewish. No, it couldn't have been because he was a totally abusive man who had a drinking problem.

No, it was because deep down, I don't think the man ever loved me and was in his heart an anti-Semite.

And it wasn't because he didn't make money for years and would hide in local bars where I thought he was actually working at a job. No, in her mind it was none of those things. The reason that P.D. and I didn't work out was that he wasn't a Jew.

Is that the craziest bit of logic?!? But actually, by that time; I was so untrusting of my taste in men, I listened to her and agreed to be listed on a Jewish online dating service. OK, now you say, "Well, I didn't think Sven is Jewish?." I will answer that with, "You're absolutely correct!"

When you ask my husband what religion he is, he often says something slightly kidding and slightly factual like, "I'm a devout musician."

He was actually raised a Southern Baptist. He has told me often that that is where he got most of his sense of humor. (I actually think we all have gotten a lot of our humor from our religion. Don't you think so?) But Sven is a type of guy who really wanted to date someone his own age (one of the many reasons why I love him so much!), and in his line of business (music); he always met younger girls. When one of his friends suggested that he join a dating service, he thought he'd give it a try.

He actually said that joining an online service was like walking down the street buck naked. It was while he was on that service that he got an invitation to join a Jewish dating service for an additional $5/month (what a deal!). Years before, he graduated from a college where many of the students were Jewish, and he had dated many Jewish women; so I think his beginning line to me when he contacted me was, "If not being Jewish is OK with you, you being Jewish is fine with me." Simply put. But when he contacted me, I figured not only was this guy not an anti-Semite, he probably had damn good taste!

A few months later, at our wedding, my friend who had signed me up for the service said, "Leave it to you, Lou, for finding the only non-Jew on a Jewish dating service and *marrying him.*"

Honestly, I rack it up to karma. Even though I was outside of my comfort zone; I would never have met the love of my life had it not been for J-Date! If that doesn't make me religious, nothing will.

PAMELA'S UNBELIEVABLY DELICIOUS "4" LAYER BAKED ALASKA

1 angel food cake
1 carton of raspberry sorbet
1 ½ gallon dark chocolate ice cream
1 ½ gallon vanilla bean ice cream
6 egg whites
1 cup of sugar
½ tbsp. vanilla
1 tbsp. cream of tartar

Take a large pie pan and lay small slices of angel food cake to cover the bottom of the pan.
Spread the slightly melted dark chocolate ice cream over the cake.
Lay small slices of angel food cake to cover the chocolate ice cream.
Spread the slightly melted raspberry sorbet over the cake.
Lay small slices of angel food cake to cover the raspberry sorbet over the cake.
Spread the slightly melted vanilla bean ice cream over the cake.
Quickly stick the ice cream pie in the freezer and let set for 2 to 3 hours.
Once completely frozen, Preheat oven to 500 degrees.
Beat 6 egg whites until it peaks. Slowly add sugar, vanilla, and cream of tartar. Beat until the meringue peaks again.
Take out the ice cream pie and place on cookie sheet. Quickly cover the entire pie with the meringue and make it as tall as possible. Place in preheated oven until all of the peaks are golden brown.
Put the pie back into the freezer for an hour.
Drizzle caramel sauce and hot fudge over the top of the pie and serve.
Enjoy!

Chapter 3

My New Official Mantra is "Woulda, Coulda, Shoulda…. Kept My Big Mouth Shut"

Yesterday could have been one of the proudest days of my life. Yes, the operative words for the moment are "could have been," and yes, it "would have been" in the top, say, 20 proudest days of my life, had I not been such an idiot and just played like a normal suburbiaville Mom and kept my big mouth shut! Yes, that is so much easier said than done, and by now, I know that you realize this flaw about me. But before you agree, please just let me tell you my sad, sad story.

Yesterday, the high school that Maggie attends had their Parent/Teacher Open House Conference. Because the high school is so huge, those in charge decided years ago that it would be easier for both the teachers and the parents if they had the open house from 3:30 p.m. to 8:00 p.m. It was set up where all the teachers sat at a desk, in alphabetical order so that they would be easy to find, and the parents would stand in line for their chance to talk to each of their kid's eight teachers for 10 minutes. They were to receive their kid's trimester Progress Report, hear about how their kid was doing in each of their classes, and see if there was something that we, as wonderful, caring parents, could do to help our child to succeed in Trigonometry or Beginning Chemistry. (Thank God I don't have to help either of our kids with their homework!)

Sounds great, doesn't it? Well, it should have been. Unfortunately, some of these parents were quite self-indulgent and decided that they needed to talk to all their child's teachers for 20 or 30 minutes. The mother and father would sit and intently talk to each of these very tired, well-meaning, but quite burnt out teachers for way too long. Let's face it, by being on your best behavior for hours, by 7:30 p.m. who wouldn't be just a wee bit sick of all of these parents who need to get a life?

As I was standing in line, eight parents deep (in my mind calculating that it will take me another 80 minutes before it's my turn), waiting for two parents to finally finish talking to this very sweet ceramics teacher; I couldn't help but ask myself, "What the hell can you talk about for 23 minutes to a ceramics teacher?" Would it go something like, "Well, Jimmy tries very hard on the pottery wheel, but his bowls just don't turn out as symmetrical as they should? What should we do to help his bowls be more round?" PLEASE, oh please, give me a "suburbiaville break!"

Maybe it was just that I was just a wee bit bitchy after a very long day at work. I woke up at 6:00 a.m. when Mollie missed her bus and I had to drive her to school in the pouring rain. Or maybe it was that I was still in my black corporate suit, not having had dinner yet, while Sven was recording a harmonica solo for a CD for some friends of his. Or just maybe it was that the girls were waiting for me to pick them up for a "jewelry party" where I had to overpay for some inexpensive jewelry so that a close friend of mine, who got talked into throwing one of these stupid "business pyramid" parties, would get a necklace that she's wanted for free?

This entire time, I could see, in my peripheral vision, hundreds of these suburban moms wearing their comfortable sweatpants and jeans, mingling and socializing, having a wonderful time catching up on all the neighborhood "scoop," while their dull husbands were doing their dutiful best to follow their wives and smile when they were supposed to.

I was starting to feel sorry for myself (I always do, especially when I'm hungry), but besides the little pity party I was beginning to have for myself, I was actually having one of the best nights I've ever had.

So now you're asking, how the heck could you be having a wonderful time when you're feeling and looking quite horrible? The "glow" was due to the fact that every review I had for my daughter up to this point of the night was wonderful.

I don't think I had been this proud of Maggie in years! There was a point when the teachers were spewing words like "a pleasure in class," "achieving a high A," "always paying attention," when I actually stopped and asked, "Excuse me, are you sure we are talking about Maggie? She is about 5'2" and has a short, strawberry blonde bob?" I didn't mean to sound flippant and I wasn't trying to sound like a smart ass; I was just in total shock.

As I've often said, though my kid is very cute and naive, she is also A.D.D, O.C.D, S-P-O-I-L-E-D, and many more acronyms used so often in this particular millennium. She also hadn't taken a drop of any medicine for years. Sven and I decided years ago that we would take her off all of those medicines that the doctors and teachers told us she needed. Though I realize that it works for millions of children, with Maggie the medicine created a bizarre "alien child" who lost a ton of weight and was crawling out of her skin most of the time. Because of that, we both decided, give us damn B's and C's, but please just give us our goofy kid back to us and we'll just deal with all of the other stuff ourselves.

Anyway, I didn't realize until I got home later that night that I had a very attractive amount of mascara running down my face from tears of sheer joy after several of these one-on-one meetings. Thank God I was nearing the end of the evening, and had only two teachers left to speak to. I actually had stood in line for about 20 minutes, realizing that I was waiting in line for the wrong "Mr. Corwin"(who would ever think that one school would have two teachers, not even related, with the same name?!)

After that debacle, I was entering the teacher conference "home stretch." I was feeling pretty good at the moment, being able to see a light at the end of the tunnel and having my Post Wonderful Report Card Glow (aka: P.W.R.C.G.) so, I guess I just got a little giddy.

Let me also say that, as I was driving to the conference, I had called Maggie and scribbled all of her teacher's names corresponding to the classes that they taught on a rumpled piece of paper that I found on the floor of my messy car. So, needless to say, it wasn't the neatest penmanship I've ever had. My handwriting isn't really that great even when I'm stationary. My handwriting is so bad that people often ask me if I had wanted to be a doctor.

Anyway, I marked off each teacher that I had already met with. I finally sat down with the second-to-last teacher on my list. This very nice, slightly balding teacher started off saying, "Maggie has been an absolute pleasure in class so far this year. Even though she currently has an 89.98935%, I'm sure she will be able to work really hard to jump over to an 'A' in the next 6 weeks."

Alas, my "glow" was continuing, and I said, "Oh, I'm thrilled to hear that! Thank you for letting me know!" Trying to sound like the aware, concerned parent that I am and trying to mimic some of these other, over-the-top obsessive parents, I continued, "Are there any extra-credit projects she can do to turn that 88.98935% to an A-?" He continued, "Well, not really, but I'm sure that she can do it with her next assignment."

The very nice teacher continued, "How is she doing with her project right now?" I said, "Well Mr. Corwin, she's doing O.K. with it, but she had a problem as to where to put the hymen on the picture of the woman last night. (Just to keep you in the loop, the class was in the portion of an assignment where each student had to draw an "anatomically correct" male and female with all their reproductive organs.)

This man's slightly balding head turned beet red. He looked at me like I had lost my damn mind. He said, "Ma'am, You do mean, "where she should put the "HYPHEN," right?, "Not the 'HYMEN'!!!"

As he looked at me unbelievably, and all of the parents standing in line behind me listening to our entire conversation, looking at me like I was the new winner of the "Most Demented Parent of the Year Award," I said, "Well, you are the health teacher, right? He looked at me, and said,

"NO LADY, I'M THE ENGLISH TEACHER!"

After I crawled out the door of the high school, drove to the house and picked up the girls to go to the jewelry party, I was still so embarrassed about the horribly stupid thing that I said to the poor, unassuming teacher. I began to tell Maggie that I had a "good news/ not-so-good news" scenario for her.

Maggie sat in fear, ready for me to "drop the proverbial ball" as I nervously rambled on. I told her how damn proud I was of all of her glowing reviews. Finally, I thought I'd better get it over with and fess up and tell her what her lovely mother did at the conference.

I wasn't sure if I would be overreacting to start packing up her messy locker and find a new school after my minor faux pas, but I knew she'd end up hearing about it from probably a slew of parents and students who have too much free time on their hands and couldn't wait to tell everyone the unbelievably ignorant thing that I had said.

I just knew that, as a responsible adult, the story must come from me. Thank God she is growing into a strange woman who is beginning to have the same twisted sense of humor I have. And actually, after she screamed in horror and told me that she'd never be able to look this teacher in the eyes again, and as tears were streaming down her face from laughing so hard, she stopped and said in almost a whisper (quite maturely, if I do say so myself!), "Mother, what possessed you in the first place to even tell Mr. Corwin that I had problems drawing the hymen??"

I looked at her and very squeamishly said, as I was shrugging my shoulders, "Well Maggie, I'm not really sure….I guess I just wanted to make small talk."

After racking my brain to think of a recipe that actually goes with this chapter, I thought that I had to do something that had cherries in it (Get it?). This is one of my cute mom's most famous and oldest recipes. I hope you'll love it.

TINKERBELL JOANIE'S CHERRIES JUBILEE

4 oranges, scooped out with top cut off and frozen (to use as the bowl)
1/2 cup sugar
2 tbsp cornstarch
1/4 cup water
1/4 cup orange juice
1 lb bing or other dark, sweet cherries, rinsed and pitted (or use frozen pitted cherries)
In a medium-size bowl, combine the orange juice, sugar, and cornstarch .
In a skillet, heat juice from cherries over moderate heat. Add cornstarch mixture. When juice thickens, add cherries to warm through. Pour in warmed liqueur, then burn off the alcohol by touching a long match to the pan. Remove cherries from heat. Scoop vanilla ice cream into the frozen oranges and spoon cherries over the ice cream.

Chapter 4

The Art Of Compromise

My husband, Sven, is probably by far the coolest, most wonderful man I've ever met. The way we met was a miracle. I think it was a cross between "FGK" (Finally Good Karma) and God saying that I had been through enough crap. It was about time for me to meet the one man who would finally love and even like the person that I am, even when I'm stepping in cow pies that I mistake for lily pads or tripping in the street and skinning my knee (which I just did tonight when we decided to take a walk after dinner).

I've already told you about the strange way we met. Too bad it took fate 44 years. I guess it's just a lesson to never take things for granted. I'm sounding a bit mature and a little Buddhist right now, aren't I? Anyway, marrying me was not an easy feat. Not only did a man in the middle of his life have to change his entire lifestyle; he actually became the father to our two little girls. I left Psycho Dick when the kids were 2 and 4 years old, so they don't really remember a time without Sven as their Daddy.

Anyway, this guy owns a wonderful, very hip record/CD/music store in the city. He and his college roommate started selling albums out of the trunks of their old cars about 30 years ago, and now they have a converted movie theater that is a nice hangout for devoted music lovers of all ages. To say that I am proud of Sven and his partner is an understatement of huge proportion.

We began our marriage with just one little compromise. He would change everything about his entire life and I wouldn't complain about his keeping his wonderful, 100-year-old house in the city that was near his store. This meant that I would never be able to quit my day job. But hell, neither can he. I actually thought that it was the least that I could do, in as much as he was altering his entire existence for me and the girls.

Let me say that having two homes does have wonderful fringe benefits. He likes to say that the house that we actually live in (the one that I bought when the girls and I were hiding from P.D.) is not big enough to hold all of his albums and CDs. Even though the house is in "Suburbiaville Hell," it is in pretty much an idyllic setting where the kids can walk to the nice and free public school, ride their bikes in the neighborhood, have Kool-Aid stands, etc.

Many people in this city (the people with money) are lucky to have several homes (especially if you're a Republican. And of course we're neither. People with money or Republican). There is a beautiful lake about 150 miles away from the city where many people who can afford to have a second condo or home along with a boat or Jet Skis. No, not us. God forbid we do what is conventional. We just decided that instead, we would have a "Democrat city house" and a "Republican county house." Sven loves to call the city house the "adult home."

After 5 years of this arrangement, I've definitely come to the realization (probably all of those business classes that I took in college) that a damn hotel once or twice a week would be a heck of a lot cheaper. But it really does allow him to decorate his own space. We don't disagree often, but when we do it usually is about my interior decorating taste. He calls all of my stuff "lawyer art," while his taste is more in line with Inca goddesses and posters of Jimi Hendrix and Sam Cooke.

OK, I'm digressing, and this is all a little embarrassing. But hey, we're adults, and I do feel as though I've already told you my deepest and darkest secrets. (You're probably saying, "Please Lou, just give it a rest.") But Sven and I are a married, full-time working couple and bringing up young kids. And luckily, are still in the "La La phase" of our relationship. Like many middle-aged couples who marry after they both have children, it's just very difficult to get away from the kids. So hell, we just try to get our money's worth out of the "adult house" as often as possible.

So, about a week ago, we were planning a romantic long lunch at the "adult house." I had picked up some salads, and he had gone over earlier to set up the candles, turn on the Marvin Gaye, light the fire, yada, yada, yada. As I was driving through his neighborhood, I saw about 20 people standing in the street. They all looked quite nice and were impeccably dressed. They also were all looking quite neighborly.

Being so excited thinking about the spontaneous rendezvous that was going to take place in a few minutes, I waved in a very friendly way to all my new hip, city neighbors. Even though they didn't know who the hell I was, I just smiled and giggled a little. I opened my window to say, "Hi, how are you? Beautiful day, isn't it?" in a sweet, Pointer Sisters "I'm So Excited, I Just Can't Hide It" kind of way. They all looked at me like I had lost my mind. I just quickly closed my window and put my dark sunglasses back on. And as I drove past all these people, I saw a long, black hearse with a huge "FUNERAL" sign on it.

I was so embarrassed, I thought I would pass out. These people probably thought, "Who the heck is this strange, bleached blonde woman, smiling and laughing during a time of such grief?" And then they probably would continue with something like, "Will someone please tell that bitch to go back to the stupid suburbs?!"

When I walked into the "adult house," I was totally red-faced. I began to tell my husband this horrific story, saying that I didn't think that I would ever be able to show my face in "his" neighborhood again. I proceeded to tell him that I probably had just ruined his reputation in his wonderful "cool community." As I was just rambling on and on about what a fool I was, and asked him if he could ever forgive me for being so stupid, Sven just looked at me and said in his quintessential deadpan style,

"Hon, don't worry about it, they just saw your car and assumed you had a brisket in your back seat!"

If you don't have a brisket in your back seat, here is another delicious and easy recipe to bring to a shiva or wake:

PATTI'S SPINACH SQUARES

Preheat the oven to 350 degrees. In a medium sized mixing bowl mix all together and place in a buttered 9 x 13 pan for 35 minutes.

2 boxes of thawed frozen chopped spinach
1 lb monterey jack cheese
4 tablespoons butter
3 eggs
1 cup flour
1 cup milk
1 tsp salt
1 tsp pepper
Let cool for a few minutes, Cut in squares and serve.

Chapter 5

Who Needs An Imagination?
(You Couldn't Make This Stuff Up –
Even If You Tried)
Part 1

Yesterday, as Mollie and I were getting out of the car to meet a few people for a late lunch, she looked at the backseat and saw a copy of my first book. She looked at me and said, "Mommy, you lied in your book." Then she quickly added casually, "Oh, by the way, Dick called last night (both she and Maggie call their "bio-dad" by his first name, which of course isn't really Dick) and said that you owe him a big, big check!"

Not even worrying about what absurd thing P.D. said, I became a little worried about our daughter reading something in my book. I decided a while back that both Maggie and Mollie are not allowed to read my first memoir until either –(1) They are 40 years old and have families of their own, or (2) I'm dead.

Let me also back up a little and tell you that P.D. blesses us every couple of months with a lovely phone call, usually a continuous spewing of mean and bizarre things. So it really didn't faze me when she told me that he called. As a prime example, let me tell you a quick story.

A few months after Sven and I got married and returned from our wonderful honeymoon, I was cooking dinner and heard Maggie in the bathroom crying. I ran in, thinking that something had happened, and said, "Honey, what is wrong?" Are you all right? She looked at me as if someone had just run over our 14-pound Chihuahua and said, "Oh Mommy, 'Dick' just called and said that Daddy…" Another FYI to my new BFFs: with absolutely no urging from either of us, the girls started calling Sven "Daddy" immediately; they didn't even wait until we were married. I think it's because we became a family so quickly, and it seemed so damn natural. I also think that at the ages they were (5 and 7), they were just in dire need of a full-time, accountable, loving-to-a-fault, no-drama and sober Daddy, and Sven was the perfect fit. Digressing for the last time in this story – I promise: I honestly think that Mollie looks more like Sven, than either me or P.D. One of these days I'll show you photos and let you be the judge!

Anyway, I was trying to find out if she was just being hormonal or if something terrible had happened. Had her little sister finally decided to wallop her in the head in return for the last week of torment she had inflicted for no apparent reason? Could it mean that the wise old saying, "Payback is such a bitch" came true? Confucius said that, didn't he?

Continuing, Maggie blurted out, "Oh Mommy, Dick said that Daddy is a black man inside a white man's body!" I just looked at her and thought, "What the heck? And furthermore, who in their right mind would say such a thing to their 8-year-old child?!?" I quickly tried to diffuse the ignorant comment and said, "Well Honey, if it is true, it definitely has many good points!" I continued in as lighthearted way as I could muster, "Daddy certainly has a lot of rhythm and can really dance." (I was also thinking of other things that wouldn't pop into her mind at all.)

She looked at me in between her tears and said, "Is it true, Mommy?" I said, in the most motherly, calming voice I could muster, even though deep down I wanted to run down to his icky one-bedroom apartment and start slapping the poop out of him, "Oh, Honey, I don't know why your Bio-Dad would say stuff like that, but you're going to have to just ignore him when he says mean and stupid things."

Hearing all the commotion and always hating to miss anything going on, Mollie ran upstairs to the bathroom, where we were having our very serious meeting, and said, "What's the matter, Maggie?" Maggie looked at her very seriously and said, "Oh, Mollie, Dick just called to tell me that Daddy is a black man inside a white man's body! Do you believe it?" Without hesitation, Mollie said, "Oh, Maggie, Dick is just a butthead."

I just looked at my youngest daughter and thought very proudly, "Boy, in seven words – this kid just nailed it!" And then I thought, "I'm going to need to buy this kid a [very inexpensive] car when she's 16 as a way of saying "thank you."

OK, so getting back to my original story... - Mollie was telling me that I had lied in my first book. Hoping and praying that she hadn't read any of it, I said, "What do you mean that I lied in my book, Honey?" I was holding my breath when she looked at me with her big brown eyes and said, "Mom, on the cover of your book, they have that picture of you. You never ever wear pink, and that dress is bright pink. You lied about your dress!". I was so relieved. I just sighed, smiled and replied, "Oh, Honey, that is just a goofy caricature of me and doesn't look like me at all." I continued, "Just think: if it was a true picture of me, I would have a much bigger tush and would be wearing a long, black jacket to cover it at all times, along with tight pants with an elastic waistband, and I'd probably have mayonnaise in my hair along with some chunk of pink lipstick on my forehead." She looked at me, giggled and said, "You're right, Mom!" And then she continued, "I guess when you write your own book, you get to pretend you look like whatever you want on the cover." I giggled too, and replied, *"Exactly!"*

I thought about it for a few seconds and asked, "So, why on Earth did Dick think that I owed him a big check?" (In the back of my mind, I was thinking that his pickled mind is mixed up about who owes who many, many big checks.) She looked at me and again smiled. "He said that a friend of his bought your book and gave it to him." She continued, "He said that he read it and said that all of the stories that you wrote about would have never happened had it not been for *him*! So, because of this, you're going to owe him millions from when you start making a lot of money and they buy the movie rights!"

I just was kind of stunned for a second. I thought, "No, he's not angry about everything I said. No, he's not saying that any of the stories were exaggerated or made-up. No, he's not calling me a liar, or that familiar loving title 'whore bitch slut' for airing dirty laundry. No, this guy that I stupidly married twice just told our daughter that he wanted to get paid for what I said about him since, I guess, I wouldn't have any of these lovely stories at all had it not been for him!"

As I said in the title of my chapter, *you can't make this stuff up* even if you tried, and who the heck needs an imagination?!

So, I wanted to give my new BFF's a recipe that I made up and I'm kind of known for. It all started when I was a teenager and liked phyllo dough so much that I experimented with it and came up with these recipes.

As a play on the name of this chapter (since it's going to be in many parts), I thought I'd give my new best friends my all-time favorite, most popular recipe in this "phyllo genre" and just tweak it for each chapter. I hope you enjoy them all!

Honestly, I think people invite me over to their parties, not just for my stunning personality, but if they are truly honest with themselves, it's really for my Crab Strudel.

CRAB STRUDEL A LA LOU

Crab Mixture:
¼ cup of butter
¼ cup of chopped celery
¼ cup of chopped onion
¼ cup of chopped mushrooms
½ teaspoon of minced garlic
salt and pepper to taste
8 oz cream cheese
2 cans of crabmeat
strudel dough:
1 stick of melted butter
6 sheets of phyllo dough (about ½ of a package)

*Put the first 6 ingredients in a large microwaveable bowl and microwave
For 2 minutes on high. Use a blender and blend in the cream cheese and
crabmeat. Refrigerate mixture for an hour.*

*Preheat oven to 350 degrees
Take ungreased cookie sheet and place one sheet of phyllo dough down,
then take a pastry brush and brush the sheet with melted butter.
Then place second sheet of dough, crumbled up a bit, and brush with butter.
Repeat four more times.
Take the Crabmeat mixture and spoon evenly in a straight line in the middle
of the dough.
Carefully fold over the strudel, folding over the two ends as if you are
wrapping a gift.
Brush the strudel with the rest of the butter and bake for 30 minutes or until
golden brown.
Cut in slices when still warm and serve.*

CHAPTER 6

Who Needs An Imagination?
(You Couldn't Make This Stuff Up -
Even If You Tried)
Part 2

I am absolutely positive that I'm in the majority when I say that my favorite novel of all time is *To Kill a Mockingbird*. In my opinion, it is the most poignant, beautiful work of art and no matter how often I read it, I pick up new things about it. It truly changed my way of thinking and my life, in so many ways.

Did you know that Harper Lee was the only author who won a Pulitzer Prize for the one and only book she ever wrote?

Harper Lee had a story to tell, and once she told it, she was "done". How beautiful is that?

Well, needless to say, I'm not anything like the greatest one-time novelist, Harper Lee. Am I hearing many of my readers 'in stereo' saying, "Duh"?!

Yes, I know, not only are my stories not poignant, but I don't think I will ever be able to stop writing about the goofy things that happen to me on a daily basis. Writing is just such wonderful therapy, and I truly hope that you, my new best friends, will get something — anything out of my stories. I would be so happy if you can find even one little anecdote to relate to that makes you either laugh or cry, or that hopefully will make you feel much better about your daily life. And hell, if that doesn't work, then at least you'll have excellent recipes to cook so you can eat yourself to oblivion. You see, Harper had her "lot in life," and I guess this may be mine.

And that leads me to my next story. I wasn't sure if I should just change the name of all of my books from "Brain Dead in The Burbs" to "Who Needs An Imagination". Instead, I'll just have several chapters with the same name and set them apart by numbering them. I hope that is all right with you and not too confusing. I just don't think any other chapter title would be appropriate.

Last night, Sven had his annual college reunion. You are probably saying to yourself, "annual college reunion?" "Hell, we have ours every 10 or 15 years?" I had thought when I first heard about these reunions, "Heck, I've never been to even one of my college reunions." And honestly, because I worked more than 40 hours a week all during my college years, I really couldn't name four people from school that I knew (unless, of course, one of them was the very handsome and 'muy macho' bartender, George (from Bowling Green, Missouri) who I worked with at the college tavern and restaurant. And, who of course wouldn't have anything to do with me. Gee, I wonder why?

OK, I'm digressing yet again. Sven was very close to many of his college friends. In fact, he still is – his old roommate has been his business partner now going on 32 years! He went to a private, fine arts college in the 70s, and the majority of students were from out of state. So, I guess Sven and many of his classmates just ended up building a bond that has lasted for close to 4 decades. It really is quite beautiful when you think about it. For the past 8 years, I've been tagging along at these reunions as Mrs. Sven, and everyone has honestly been very sweet, accepting me and letting me join their little group.

The day of the reunion, Sven mistakenly called another friend of his, who is a great guy and the owner of the most unusual bar/restaurant I've ever been to. I love it. When you walk in — and I don't know why this happens, but something will come over you that automatically makes you just want to say, "Toto, we're not in Kansas anymore!"

Anyway, the guy said, "Hey Sven, I'm glad you called me. It's so weird, because I was just going to call you, but you beat me to it!" He continued, "A few cousins of one of your old art teacher's (a man who had passed away about 5 years ago) came by and dropped off a ton of art that he had done before he died. I took the few pieces that I wanted to keep, but didn't know what I should do with the rest…, I decided that I'm going to give it all away to anyone who wants it tomorrow afternoon at 2:00 p.m., but wanted you to come by and take what you'd like first."

Sven was thrilled. He had absolutely loved this teacher. Have you ever had a college professor that everyone loved? Someone whose classes were completely filled, even if the students had to sit on the floor? A professor who was so enigmatic that the students would listen intently to every word he or she said? Well, that was what this professor was like. He was such a great and popular teacher. He even took many of his students on trips during the summer to visit art museums throughout the country.

This professor happened to have a disease called gigantism. I know very little about it (actually, this was the first time I had ever really heard of anyone who had it). But what Sven told me is that it is a rare genetic disease that occurs in Eastern Europe and that, whereas most of the people who have it are feeble-minded, approximately 2 percent of its victims are "off the chart" genius. Are you familiar with the saying that "the closer you are to genius, the closer you are to insanity"? (Please remember this for the end of the story, all right?). Sven told me that this man's wife was a deeply religious woman who was a missionary, and they never had children, probably because of his genetic condition.

So, we had a lovely evening with his reunion buddies, and then at about 11:00 p.m., we headed downtown to this huge warehouse that was connected to the restaurant/bar. We told our daughter Maggie, who happened to be at a friend's home, that we would pick her up as soon as we could, but we had to run a little errand first.

I don't know why, but in my feeble little mind, I was thinking, "Oh, my God. We'll take a few of his paintings and replace the "lawyer art" (that's what Sven calls all of my abstract watercolor paintings in the suburbiaville home). And then, when we're tired of it or need a little financial windfall, we'll just take a little field trip to the PBS television show, "Antiques Roadshow" and I'll act surprised when they tell me that we are in possession of $2,000,000 worth of art! Sounded like a great plan, didn't it?

Well, we walked in, and here I am with three men besides Sven; and, as God is my witness, there were over 200 pieces of gigantic — I don't know how else to explain it — penis pictures. The one exception was a room-size painting titled "Holes;" and of course it showed hundreds of variations of charcoal drawings of vaginas. Not your normal, run-of-the-mill "vagina painting," mind you. This one depicted each vagina covered by its own distinct type of window treatment (blinds, curtains, shutters and so forth). The art had that kind of interactive feeling where you could open and close the blinds or curtains whenever you wanted to.

I was trying to be as cool as I could, especially in front of all of these men. I tried to rationalize that maybe this artist had just been in his "penis period." Perhaps *The New York Times* art critic would call it "the P to the Second Power Period." Who the hell knows? But deep down, I wanted to run out of there screaming like Jeff Goldblum did in the movie, "The Fly"; "Help Meeeeeeeeeee."

My smart-ass Sven thought it was hilarious. He was like, "Oh Hon, look at this piece. It would be perfect right over our fireplace, don't you think?" Finally, I gave up and decided that this was one of those days that I'm thrilled that he kept his "city house." I finally was able to say, "It's late. We have to pick up Maggie. Just pick out something you want for your home, something that Maggie and Mollie will never have to see, and we're out of here!"

He picked out a piece of furniture. Did I tell you that this artist also made furniture? And did I also tell you that not only did he have a sex fixation, but it also ran the gamut with religion, as well! (This may have stemmed from his wife being a missionary. Who the heck knows?!) All I know is that, at 12:30 a.m. on a Friday night, I was walking down a very dark downtown street, helping Sven carry a huge coffee table in the shape of a religious cross with a humongous penis attached to it.

To add insult to injury, not only did it take us about a half-hour to fit the thing in Sven's car, but as we were driving to the suburbs, this "art" was so damn big that the penis kept hitting me in the face. (Don't you just hate when that happens?) I really didn't know if I wanted to laugh or cry; but then, of course, it got worse.

How, you may be asking yourself, can it possibly be worse than this? (Talk about needing an imagination?!?)

Well, I'll tell you how. When we finally got to the home of Maggie's friend, it was so late that the very sweet Catholic and very conservative mother and her daughter, who had waited for hours for Maggie to be picked up, walked Maggie to the car. When Maggie opened the car door, all three of them saw what was inside. The mom screamed and looked at both Sven and me in total horror.

I don't think words could ever explain the humiliation and feeling of sheer defeat that I felt in that moment. I knew in that one instant that I, Laura Ray, will never fit in in Suburbiaville.

I want you to know that I have no imagination at all; and honestly, I couldn't make these stories up even if I tried.

I thought long and hard (no pun intended…) about what recipe would fit this chapter, and I decided to go with a strudel theme. I hope you enjoy it and you can shape it in the shape of a penis, only if you'd like!

SPINACH STRUDEL A LA BOO

(AKA: A delicious version and so easy version of Spanakopeta)
Spinach Mixture:
¼ cup of butter
2 thawed drained boxes of frozen spinach
¼ cup of chopped celery
¼ cup of chopped onion
½ teaspoon of minced garlic
2-8 oz cream cheese
½ cup of grated parmesan cheese
salt and pepper to taste

Strudel Dough:
1 stick of melted butter
6 sheets of phyllo dough (about ½ of a package)

Put the first 6 ingredients in a large microwaveable bowl and microwave
for 2 minutes on high. Use a blender and blend in the cream cheese and
crabmeat. Refrigerate mixture for an hour.
Preheat oven to 350 degrees.
Take ungreased cookie sheet and place one sheet of Phyllo dough down,
Then take a pastry brush and brush the sheet with melted butter.
Then place second sheet of dough, crumbled up a bit, and brush with butter.
Repeat four more times.
Take the Crabmeat mixture and spoon evenly in a straight line in the middle
of the dough. Carefully fold over the strudel, folding over the two ends as if
you are wrapping a gift.
Brush the strudel with the rest of the butter and bake for 30 minutes or until
golden brown.
Cut in slices when still warm and serve.
(This recipe makes two medium size penis-shaped strudels)

CHAPTER 7

Who Needs An Imagination?
(You Couldn't Make This Stuff Up -
Even If You Tried)
Part 3

Have you ever seen those bumper stickers that say, "Where are all of those flashbacks they promised me in the 70s"? Besides the ones that say, "I still blame Yoko Ono" or "If you don't like my driving, stay off the sidewalk," I think the flashback one probably wins the prize as my favorite bumper sticker of all time. It always makes me giggle, and telling you this story that happened only a few days ago will do just that. I'm actually giggling as I'm writing this. I'll try my best to bring justice to it. And I believe that the entire story is solid proof that you don't have to be an ex-hallucinogen taker to experience such strange occurrences on an almost daily basis. All you have to do is to have the name "Laura Ray".

Let me begin by reiterating that Sven is a huge World Music enthusiast. So much so that he has been asked from time to time to be one of the many emcees at a very impressive music festival in Northern California. From the time that I met him, I always knew that, come early summer, Sven just had to make this yearly pilgrimage up to the mountains. It wasn't that he merely had to attend; it was more of a calling that he is just unable to ignore, if you know what I mean. He never wanted to take me because he thought that I would just hate it. My dear friend Ellie Grossman Cohen, who happens to be a fellow author of a hilarious series called Mishegas of Motherhood, has devoted an entire chapter to the fact that "Jewish Women Don't Camp." I guess my husband must have read her book and was afraid to take the chance of seeing a completely different, and not very pretty side of me. (Or he must have remembered that story of mine where I mistook cow pies for lily pads — one teeny tiny mistake that will haunt me forever.)

Anyway, last year the music line up was especially fantastic, and when Sven was asked to emcee the set of one of the headliners, we both decided I would take the plunge and go together. It was during summer break, the kids were at their 5-week summer session of "Camp Sheryl" (my sister-in-law's home down South), and I talked my boss into allowing me to take a few much-needed days off of work. (I actually think he knew that if I didn't take some time off, I would totally lose it.)

We ended up having the best time. I was so darn proud of my semi-celebrity husband, and there really isn't anything sweeter than romantic, "even-I-can-dance-to it" reggae music. I found everyone at the festival to be so sweet. It was very family oriented; and, unlike many rock concerts and sporting events that I've been to in the Midwest, no one ever gets drunk and stupid, or picks a fight, or pukes or pees all over their team or multiple fans. No, surprisingly, I very often found myself standing behind gorgeous 20-something females who never even heard of my old standby lingerie, "Spanx," and who had perfect complexions that never require any makeup. Why is it that they all happen to have names like "Sky Dancer" or "Jah Princess Moonbeam"? The food lines were all for jerk chicken, fried plantains, and tofu burgers. How remarkably peaceful and healthy is that?

I had so much fun at the festival that year that both Sven and I knew that he was stuck, and there would be no way that I'd ever let him go to this annual event without me ever again! Poor guy. Some men get to go on hunting and fishing trips or even to Las Vegas with their buddies. Not my man, he just always looked forward to going to the festival with all of his other reggae fanatic friends, and now he has to drag me along with him.

This year, the 3-day festival ended on Sunday. It was even better than the year before, and because last year's was so amazing, I thought that would be impossible. The weather up in the mountains was so beautiful, but it was pretty cold. We ended up having to go to a secondhand store to buy some warm clothes because all we packed was summer stuff. Otherwise the lineup was fantastic, and somehow Sven's photo even made it into the program. Life couldn't be sweeter! So, you may ask, "What is so weird about this scenario? Well, I'll try to explain in as much detail as I can. (I don't entirely trust my memory because I think that I tend to subliminally repress strange things that happen to me — especially when they end up taking years off of my life span)

One of Sven's friends, who could probably be knighted as "Sir Reggae Nerd," had asked Sven to appear on the local public radio show that night to interview the singer/songwriter who Sven had emceed for. (The show began at midnight, and remember, I'm very old and usually can't even stay up to see my favorite shows, Jon Stewart and Stephen Colbert).

Sven was particularly excited because he's been a host for our city's public radio station for over 20 years, and he happens to be a huge advocate for any city that does the same thing. He was also excited about being able to "talk up" his favorite reggae artist, who Sven feels doesn't get his just due in the U.S. So, when he asked me if it would be all right, I couldn't say anything but, "Yes Honey, of course. That sounds great!" (I know that you're saying, "Wow, that Laura Ray is such a selfless, good wife…Right?)

Well, the minute I said "Yes" and Sven confirmed with Sir Nerd that I gave him permission, our oldest (and a bit neurotic) daughter called me on my cell phone. I said, "Hi, Honey! Boy, do I miss you!" "How's Camp Sheryl?" "Did you try any other 'country foods' today?" (Our daughters think they are the first ones to have recognized the deliciousness of fried okra and fried squash — one of my sister-in-law's specialties.) Maggie basically ignored all of my stupid questions and said, "Mommy, I have to tell you something and it's really, really important!" She sounded like she was going to cry, so I asked, "Honey, what is it?" She said, "Mommy, I'm just having some terrible feelings that something really, really bad is going to happen to you and Daddy in the next few minutes!" She took a huge breath and then said, "It's scaring me so much, I don't know why I'm having these horrible feelings, but please, go home now and don't do anything else tonight at all!"

I felt horrible for our sweet, little, neurotic child. I said, "Maggie, please don't worry about us at all. Daddy and I are actually going to a radio station so that Daddy can be interviewed. Isn't that cool?!?" It was like our daughter could not care less that approximately 9 people would get to hear her father on a Godforsaken radio show in the middle of the night, talking about music that peaked in the late 1970s. (What is with these kids nowadays?). She continued, "Mommy, pleeeeease don't go! I'm telling you, something really bad is going to happen. You have to believe me!"

I quietly told our daughter, as sweetly as I could muster, that she needed to go to sleep and of course reassured her that her thoughts were silly, and that of course nothing would ever happen to us.

As God is my witness, the absolute millisecond that I got off the phone with her, a man who I never saw before jumped into the backseat of our car. (I later found out that he was a bonafide member of the Reggae Nerd Posse.) I looked at Sven, just a wee bit perplexed, and Sven looked at this man and very nonchalantly said, "Hey, you riding with us?" The guy looked at me and in a very strange spacey Californian drawl, he said, "Well, people call me 'Pigeon Boy'." He continued, "And 'Jah Bob' told me to ride with you to show you where the radio station was. He didn't want you two Midwesterners to get lost!" Sven shrugged his shoulders and I said, "Well, thank you Pigeon Boy!" I just thought to myself, "Boy, if I could just count how many times I've said, 'Thank you Pigeon Boy" in my lifetime"? As we were driving in the middle of absolutely nowhere, Sven and I tried to make small talk with Mr. Pigeon Boy. What else do you do when a complete stranger is in the backseat of your rental car at midnight? So, I began to do what I do so well, and that is to ask completely inane and stupid questions just to get the conversation rolling. (What can I say? It's a gift I've been given!)

Pigeon Boy didn't respond to any of my 18 rapid-fire questions. So then, Sven tried to ask him a few more "on-point and manly'" type of questions. Pigeon Boy didn't respond to him, either.

He was kind of an equal-opportunity uncommunicative Pigeon Boy. Finally, Sven decided to just get to the point, and he said, "So, are you back there or did we lose you?"

Complete silence. I was a nervous wreck. I was so afraid to even look back to see if he was there, and what the heck he was doing back there? My imagination just went wild. Sven even started to whistle nervously and, at the same time, I looked out the window and realized that we were in the middle of the California mountain forest. We were in the middle of frigging nowhere.

You know, the place where 98.9% of all of those people on America's Most Wanted end up being found! And the really creepy thing about it was that the radio station that we were listening to started to get real staticky, and that was the station that we were supposedly driving to! What the heck is wrong with this picture?!

Then the worst thing that could have happened, did. I looked out the window, and guess what I saw? An old, decrepit sawmill! Yep, right out of "The Blair Witch Project" or "Saw." The only thing that I could think of was, "Dammit, Maggie was right! We ARE going to die!" All along, I thought our beautiful, strawberry blonde daughter with perfect features (don't ask me how) was neurotic and just a wee bit obsessive-compulsive. Hell no, she's not PSYCHO, she's actually PSYCHIC! And who, may I ask, with this deaf mute in the backseat of our car getting ready to kill us, is the frigging idiot who didn't believe her? That would be her stupid, and now very dead, mother!

It seemed like an eternity. I kept on thinking that Pigeon Boy must be in the backseat in "ready to shred" condition with some kind of hatchet. And then, out of the blue, in the most normal tone of voice, he said, "Hey, I think we're lost. Turn around past the sawmill and make a left at that weeping willow." Sven and I both just sighed the biggest sigh of relief in stereo and pretended that everything was A-OK, that neither of us had just clearly seen our entire lives flash before our very eyes, and said, "OK Pigeon Boy. That's a great idea."

So, we finally arrived at the two-room radio station. I, of course, having almost had a full-blown coronary, had to pee as soon as I walked in. Just to tell you how backward this station was, a huge sign over the toilet said, "Only Women Please. Men, Please Pee Outside."

Two other world music obsessed nerds had beaten us there, a man who called himself "Jah Bob" and a woman who called herself "Sistah Uplift." (Once again, let me say that I couldn't make this stuff up, even if I tried!) I was ready to change my name to "Sistah Who Needs A Valium and Is Trying to Keep a Straight Face."

Sven kept looking at me, because he knew that I was biting my lip really hard to keep from laughing. These music fans were so earnestly trying to put on a great show (that probably no one in their right mind was listening to in the wee hours of the morning), and no matter what they did, it was incorrect. They took turns airing songs, explaining to their adoring fans in detail when the song originally came out, who wrote it, and so forth, and not once (for over an hour) did they get it right! As much as Sven enjoyed looking at me, I really enjoyed looking at his reaction even more. It was hilarious, and kind of sweet — in a goofy, yet well-meaning way. After the deejays fumbled on the songs, I guess they could not care less that they were giving their 9 adoring fans totally wrong information. They just started dancing in full "Rasta force" around the cramped room, dodging all the sound equipment. I've seen way too many oddball things in my life, but this really could have won in the "Top 10 Wouldn't Believe It Until You See It" award.

When we finally got back to our heated cabin at around 4:00 a.m., both collapsing in the very uncomfortable bed, Sven looked at me and said, "Honey, I bet you would have never had this kind of night had you married a stockbroker."

What can I say? My man Sven is always right.

So, if you haven't realized it yet, I wanted to have the same theme going with all of my "Who Needs An Imagination" chapters. They are all similar, but with a different twist. This strudel is absolutely delicious and everyone will be impressed with it, even though it's so darn easy to make. Enjoy, Sistahs!

SISTAH WENDY'S CHERRY CHEESE STRUDEL

Cheese Mixture:
1-1/2 8 oz. pkgs. cream cheese
3/4 cup sugar
1/2 tsp. vanilla
1 medium size can (10 oz.) cherry pie filling

Strudel Dough:
1 stick of melted butter
8 sheets of phyllo dough (about 1/2 of a package)

Preheat oven to 350 degrees
Blend the first 3 ingredients and refrigerate the cream cheese mixture for 10 minutes.
Place one sheet of phyllo dough on an ungreased cookie sheet. Then use a pastry brush to brush the sheet with the melted butter. Then lay a second sheet of dough, crumbled up a bit, and brush it with butter.
Repeat 6 more times.
Spoon the cream cheese mixture and spread with knife evenly in a straight line in the middle of the dough. Spoon cherry pie filling on top of the cream cheese mixture. Carefully fold over the strudel, folding over the two ends as if you are wrapping a gift. Brush the strudel with the rest of the butter and bake for 30 minutes or until golden brown.

Cut in slices when still warm and serve. Top with vanilla ice cream if you want to go crazy!

Chapter 8

Am I Green with Jealousy or Just Angry at Myself?

After driving Maggie and Mollie to school due to them missing the schoolbus by 22 seconds, I tripped on my raincoat walking up the stairs at 6:48 a.m. with my hair flying in a zillion directions, looking as though the house and I both were in the middle of one of the 27 tornadoes that hit the Midwest this year. I was still in my pajamas, hadn't even brushed my teeth yet, and then, in the corner of my eye, I saw three huge dog turds in our lovely living room (from of course, the rescued *almost* housebroken Chihuahua that our daughters swore to us they would take care of). And digressing again, Sven always claimed that saying that a puppy is "almost housebroken" is almost as inane as saying that a woman is *almost pregnant*. Don't ask me why, but a sudden wave of guilt overwhelmed my entire being.

You see, unbeknownst to them, I had been holding a horrible grudge for over 8 years against the "perfect couple." These particular friends of Sven happen to be a sweet, politically correct, every-which-way "green" couple who were able to retire happily at the ripe old age of 55.

They are the type of people who grow their own perfect vegetables, brew their own beer, squeeze their home-grown fresh oranges, and most probably manufacture their own air.

And yet they still have time to travel around the country to their favorite music, art, and who knows — transcendental meditation festivals after they have painstakingly plotted a roadmap indicating the most environmentally friendly route for their monthly treks.

Why, you ask, do these people have so much time, money, and energy to do all of these fabulous things? Why do they always look like they have spent hours putting together the perfect outfits to match whatever event they happen to be attending? Well, the answer is easy, and if I were mimicking Sven at this moment, I'd be screaming "*Of course they are happy: they don't have children!*"

I always thought that the reason I didn't like them was that they were smug and boring. I remember hating every minute of a nice dinner party that they threw for 3 couples. I could envision them preparing for the party by first having a 5-day long, uninterrupted conversation with each other, preparing a flow chart to decide which guests would mesh best with each other in both political and religious conversations.

We were sitting on their veranda (which of course they built with their own four hands), and my cell phone vibrated every 2 minutes because of the nonstop calls from Maggie and Mollie. All their messages were about who hit who, who has a black eye, who didn't do the dishes which they were supposed to do, who called who fat and ugly—yadda- yadda, frigging yadda.

As I was listening to all these charming messages, Sven said something a wee bit snide about how it was impossible for us to get away for even an hour without the girls driving us crazy. I guess I was giving the man I love a look that could kill, while Veronica (one-half of the perfect couple) looked at me and said, "Oh, my Dear, is something wrong between the 2 of you?"

I don't know what came over me, but, all of a sudden I just snapped and said, "Oh, I guess sometimes there are problems between 'The Cracker and the Jew! (Cracker would be Sven — who is originally from North Florida.)

Oh, my God. What the hell just came out of my mouth at this lovely, eco-friendly dinner party? I swear I'm really not one of those horrible name-calling people! The only explanation that I can possibly come up with is that our daughters have finally driven me to the brink of ickyness.

Silence suddenly came over the veranda, and then one of the men felt the need to break the uncomfortable lull and said something like, "Could you please pass that delicious homemade hummus from the garbanzo beans that you grew?"

So, getting back to this morning. At 6:49 a.m., I had just endured one of the biggest catfights I had ever witnessed between two teenage sisters. Sven and I had had to figure out whether concussions were something to be considered. And if we had decided to take them to the emergency room for head X-rays and tell the physicians what had happened, would the suburbiaville police department come and take away the spoiled little princesses who we so painstakingly raised for the last 16 years? (You know, those little questions that parents of teenagers have to ask themselves).

It was at that moment that I humbly realized that I had to apologize to the perfect couple, who had no clue how I have resented them all these years. So, here it goes. I'll let you read it before I mail it out.

Dear Vernonica and Hans,

Please accept my apology for my envy of your lifestyle. I apologize for the not-so-nice thoughts I've had over the last 8 years. I know that it was my choice to have children, as it was your choice not to have children. I understand that, and I will do my very best to not be jealous of your perfect, stress-free, rich, and oh-so-organized life. I am aware that this wave of jealousy will leave my body the moment our daughters grow out of their teens, shed their alien bodies, move out of our home, go to college, lead productive lives, get married, and then bring their gorgeous children (our grandchildren) to our home to be spoiled and then given back.

But for now, I must say that I am ashamed of my thoughts and my behavior. Perhaps aliens have taken over my body as well.

Please forgive me.

Yours truly,

Laura Ray

Now that I've gotten this off my chest, I will give you a quick and easy recipe that everyone thinks has taken me hours to prepare. You can use the avocados that you grew yourself in your gorgeous, huge garden — but if you do, please don't tell me.

FIVE-MINUTE DELICIOUS GUACAMOLE FOR PEOPLE WHO DON'T HAVE ANY TIME AT ALL

5 large, peeled avocados, chopped in medium-size chunks
½ cup chopped onion
2 tbsp chopped cilantro
½ cup Pace chunky medium picante sauce
Mix together, chill, and serve with your favorite tortilla chips.

Chapter 9

You Know You Are in Dire Need of a Vacation When....

You know you need a vacation when you are really looking forward to the colonoscopy that's scheduled for next week. Now, I've said it, and Oh My God, does that sound absolutely pathetic, or what?

What the heck is wrong with us women nowadays? I don't know why, but lately I've been a little envious of friends who are having hysterectomies. I had mine about 4 years ago in my 40s, after having my kids and in the middle of the 10-year adventure that doctors call "peri-menopause." This was after they found a 6-pound benign tumor that I later named "Fred." Getting the hysterectomy was probably one of the best things I've ever done, by far. It's amazing what not having a monthly 10-day period does to your well-being, and I'm not even talking about what it does for your love life! My favorite part of the entire adventure was, of course, after they told me that "Fred" was benign and before I felt like a small truck had run over me on the second day of recovery. My next-favorite thing was the time spent unconscious — about 5 hours —in the presence of the very handsome anesthesiologist.

I think that is when I had a small "a-ha" moment. I realized that this state of sleep was what Michael Jackson had hired that horrible doctor for. How much is it worth to have a deep, uninterrupted sleep, where your dreams come alive in full HD-TV full-screen color and surround sound? How much is it worth when you are able to zone out the kids screaming at each other— calling each other fat and ugly— and the dogs shaking their noisy collars, letting you know that they have to pee and wanting their breakfast; and the phone ringing as terror goes through your body when you find out that your boss is on the other end of the line, wanting to discuss how you are possibly going to sell another $45,692 of product in the next 3 days; and your husband is telling you that the hot tub is broken, the pool needs to be closed, 6 of our friends are coming over for dinner on Wednesday, and I have to be "more consistent" when it comes to disciplining our 2 hormonally charged, "fighting clown" daughters. It all makes that small $2,500 anesthesiology bill well worth it, don't you think?

I'm only going to admit this to my new best friends, because I think you're the only ones who will really get it. Sometimes, I find myself daydreaming about how painful it would be to have my big toe run over by a small, "kinder and gentler" truck. Nothing major, I promise — I haven't gotten that desperate. But would it be worth it to have just a teensy surgery that would require putting me "under" for just a few hours?

I realized I wasn't alone, and it just tickled the heck out of me yesterday afternoon, while I was on a 4-hour Saturday field trip — with a group of wonderful, well-meaning women — to deliver goody-filled baskets to a home for underprivileged girls. I was in the back seat on the 1-1/2 hour drive and found myself fielding about 30 phone calls from my 2 crying, fighting teenagers, along with several calls from Sven, telling me that the girls were out of control and that he was going to get the heck out of the line of fire and go out for a peaceful, Indian lunch. I found myself blurting out in front of my new friends, not really caring what they would think of me after I said it, "God, do you ever wish for minor surgery just so that you can be 'put out' for a few hours?"

The driver, a very beautiful woman who is a full-time piano teacher, mother, wife, and new first-time grandmother, turned around for a second to look at me, and without a moment of hesitation, she said, "Oh, Laura, have a colonoscopy!" She continued, "It's a perfect solution. Not only do you get a solid 2 hours of uninterrupted sleep, but when you wake up you've lost 3 pounds from all that icky prep work you had to do. It's fabulous!"

It just tickled the heck out of me, and actually it reassured me that I haven't totally lost it and become some sort of a masochist, wanting to hide in the most powerful way. Here was this gorgeous, intelligent woman telling me that she had thought about this and came up with this multi-tasking solution without even being aware of it. How amazing is that?

The only way I can end this chapter is in summary.

We, the Women of the Millennium, are just unbelievable and become even more resourceful each and every day— whether we want to or not.

(Note: As we were laughing in the car to the point where tears were streaming down our faces about how insane our lives have become, I asked my friend if it was all right to write about our crazy conversation. She said, "Of course, Laura. I'd be honored to be in your new book." Then I thought about it and said, "Well, I've got a problem: how am I ever going to tie a recipe to a colonoscopy? That's going to be really disgusting!" This very proper, perfectly dressed new friend of mine just looked at me and said, "No worries, Laura, I've got one that will fit in perfectly."

I don't need to say a word about how this recipe fits this chapter.

DR. ALEX'S CHOCOLATE ESPRESSO BEAN FUDGY CUPCAKES

1 package chocolate fudge cake mix
1 cup water
½ cup vegetable oil
3 eggs
2 tbsp of instant espresso coffee powder

Preheat oven to 350 degrees.
Beat cake mix, water, oil, and eggs in large bowl on low speed for 30 seconds, then on medium speed for 2 minutes, scraping bowl occasionally. Line a cupcake tin with pleated papers and fill each 2/3 full. Bake for 15 to 20 minutes.

Ingredients for the filling:
1 container (8 oz) of mascarpone cheese
2 tsp of milk
2 tbsp of instant espresso coffee powder
1 cup of powdered sugar

Blend and set aside.
Once cupcakes are baked, cool them for 5 minutes and then poke 1 big hole in the baked cupcakes while they are still warm, and pipe the filling into each cupcake.
When they have cooled, frost each cupcake with 1 tsp of instant espresso coffee powder mixed with 1 container of whipped-style milk chocolate frosting.
Garnish each cupcake with chocolate-covered espresso beans.
Enjoy!

Chapter 10

Could There Ever Be a More Stupid Reason to Have An Argument?

So, do you ever dream about what you would do if you ever win the Powerball? Do you know exactly how you would divvy up all the money? I just want you all to know that I would quickly pay off the mortgage for every single person I like. Wouldn't that just make everyone's life so much easier, if you didn't have a house payment to worry about every month? Or how about the dream that Johnny Depp had suddenly decided to leave his long-time girlfriend after he saw you at a Fleming's Happy Hour (which, in my humble opinion is by far the best Happy Hour in the world) and told you that he knew that you and he were soul mates? Well, none of these farfetched dreams have ever entered my mind (or have they?). But I, Laura Ray have an even more absurd dream.

My dream is that one day in the not-so-distant future, some Hollywood producer is going to call me one morning and tell me that he had just finished reading one of my books and would very much like to make a movie based on it. That dream is the subject of this chapter.

One Sunday, Sven and I were watching our favorite morning show, CBS Sunday Morning with Charles Osgood (which I always call the "Kinder, Gentler, Artsy-Fartsy 60 Minutes"). And if you are one of the lucky ones who can sleep past 8:00 a.m. on a Sunday morning without hormonal teens or overweight Chihuahuas jumping on you, I would really suggest that you record this. It's a fine show, and I've been watching it for years and years.

Anyway, in between commercials and running into the kitchen to refill our coffee cups with Sven's delicious coffee, I decided to come clean and tell Sven what my dream was.

He looked at me and chuckled a little and then said, in the dry way he always does, "That's a great idea, Doll." He continued, "I'm sure it will be a huge hit. But tell me: who do you think should play you?"

I looked at him, and thought, "How the heck can he even ask me that?" It is the quintessential "duh" question! "Well, Michelle Pfeiffer of course!" I said almost flippantly. Without a moment's hesitation, the man of my dreams, the man I love so much, the man I'm planning on spending the rest of my life with, looked at me and said, as he was spitting out his coffee, "Oh, Honey. No way. You must be dreaming!, I would think that the only actress that could possibly play you is Bette Midler!" And then the jerk continued, "And if you want your little movie to be made soon, you'd better call her today, because I heard she's got a very popular show in Vegas right now."

I looked at him as if he had 3 heads growing out of his butt and said, "You are soooo wrong!" "The only damn reason why you are picking her is because she's Jewish and over 50, and you can't think of any other older bleached blonde."

Please don't get me wrong at all. I absolutely love Bette Midler. Not only did her movie "Beaches" clearly make it on my list of the "Top 10 Chick Movies of All Time," but I think she's brilliant, talented, and beautiful. I even went so far as to boycott any movie, or really bad made-for-television movie, that is on only at 3:30 a.m., when you can't sleep and when that mean actor Ken Wahl has any part.

For those out there who do not admit to having a *People* Magazine addiction, I'll quickly explain myself. Years ago, I think in the 80s, Bette (as long as she's going to play me in the movie, we may as well be on a first-name basis, don't you think?) was in a movie called "Jinxed." I believe of course through the information I got from my Hollywood bible. I always ask myself (not often), why is it that I wouldn't be caught dead reading the *National Enquirer, Star,* or that disgusting *Globe* rag, but I'll end up quoting articles that I've read in *People* as though they are 100% true? (Just another little side note: my sister Gwendolyn was afflicted with the same addiction, until she told me that she had to cancel her subscription when she read our favorite section of the magazine, called "Passages." For those of you who are not *People* readers, it's the section that talks about who got married, who got divorced, why Charlie Sheen or Lindsay Lohan got arrested, who was born, who died, and so forth).

Well, that week's edition gave top billing to the fact that Tori Spelling's dog "Poo Poo" or "Foo Foo" or whatever had died. What made it so damn appalling is that this made top billing over the fact that Corazon Aquino, the first woman ever to become president of the Philippines, had passed away. Gwendolyn called me and said, "That's it, Lou!" She began to take short breaths — almost to hyperventilation — saying, "I can't help it. I've got to cancel my subscription! I have to make a protest in my own way and tell these people how crazy our world is becoming with celebrity frenzy!" She went on, "How the hell can they give Foo Foo top billing over President Corazon Aquino?" My sweet sister finally calmed down when she realized that she would be doing something in her own small way to protest the insanity.

OK, yes, I'm digressing again and I'll hurry up and get to the point. According to the people at *People*, Ken Wahl — and for that matter, the director of the movie — were both so mean and nasty to Bette during the filming of the movie that it caused the woman to have a nervous breakdown. So, for my own little protest against "meanness and nastiness" in Hollywood, I haven't watched anything that Wahl appears in (not that I'm missing much of anything. I think that the last time I ever even saw anything about the big jerk was when he was married to 2 different Playboy bunnies with the same name, Bitsy or Buffy or something, at the same time. Oooooh, Baby!)

So, now you know that I admire Bette Midler. But, you know how people see themselves as something totally different than how others see them? I actually saw myself as a Michelle Pfeiffer, or a bleached blonde and a little heavier Sandra Bullock, or even Goldie Hawn (you know the song, "Goldie Hawn is half-Jewish, and Paul Newman is, too, and together they make one fine looking Jew!"). I definitely didn't see myself as a Bette Midler. I guess I should have felt lucky that the love of my life didn't think of Joan Rivers, Phyllis Diller, or even Golda Meir (i.e., any older Jewish woman he could think of).

So, then I got a little nasty on that Sunday morning. I know that may shock my readers. You're probably saying, "Oh, Laura, not you! "You don't have a bitchy bone in your body, do you?" Wrong! I can be absolutely a horrible bitch, especially when dealing with my very fragile ego.

I looked at him. "OK fine then. Who do you think should play you?" I continued to spew, "How about Vincent Price? Oh yeah, I forgot: he's dead. OK, then, how about Raul Julia? Oh, no: dead." (I heard he was a great guy. I think that was in *People* Magazine, too.)

Sven just looked at me as if I had totally lost my mind. I think he was in a very small state of shock. I don't think he'd ever seen me like this before. The look of horror on his face made me finally snap out of it, and I thought, "Oh, my God, I have totally lost it! What is happening to me? How can we even be fighting over something as ignorant as this? It was then when I must have come back to reality, and if I could have snapped my fingers to make what just happened go away, I'd be snapping away.

I went up to him, as if I were carrying a white flag of surrender, put my arms around him and said, "OK, Honey. I promise not to tell anyone what just happened if you promise you won't either. Deal?

So that's what we did.

Thank God neither of us ever breathed a word about that stupid fight. I'd be so darn humiliated if anyone ever found out how ignorant I was.

Here is a recipe that can be served during the Academy Awards as you are watching me get the award for Best Original Screenplay:

HOLLYWOOD'S CHEESE BALL RECIPE a la SCHMOO

1 cup mayonnaise
1/2 cup finely chopped green onions
6 oz shredded sharp cheddar cheese
12 oz cooked bacon, crumbled
3 oz slivered almonds

Mix all ingredients and form into large ball. Chill well before serving.
Serve with your favorite gourmet crackers

CHAPTER 11

Dead Neighbors
According to Laura Ray

Let me first explain the running joke that Sven and I have shared since we got married. Do you remember me talking about the last few boyfriends I had before I totally lucked into meeting the only non-Jew on a Jewish on-line dating service that my friend "Ms. Super Jew" enrolled me in?

Well, right after I first met Sven and realized that I was falling madly in love with him, "Elliott" (once again — all names have been changed to protect those un-neurotic, not self-obsessed, strange psychiatrists out there) called me to see if he could possibly woo me back. He had done it so many times in that sad year and a half when I was still in my masochistic phase, that when I told him that I was in love with someone else and that we were going to probably be getting married, he actually screamed into the phone, "OK Laura. I just want you to know one thing. You are dead to me!"

I think I was a little stunned, and just stared at the phone for about 3 minutes. I guess that's a trait of what Farmer Jews do when someone they have been intimate with, tells them that they've been declared dead. As an fyi to those who didn't read or remember my first book, this ex-boyfriend of mine was from New York and his entire family were all very small and petite people with no one weighing over 110 lbs., including the men. To deflate my ego just a little more, his uncle referred to me as a Farmer Jew due to my height and weight. A little harsh, don't you think?

I mean, hell, Psycho Dick (P.D.) called me a whore, slut, bitch, and so forth, on a daily basis, but I don't ever think he ever called me "dead." Here, I really thought this man would honestly feel happiness for my great luck in finding the love of my life after he broke up with me for the hundredth time. Or maybe he would feel like he had done a mitzvah by releasing me from his little mind-games and allowing me to move on.

Anyway, I was a little taken aback by it, quickly hung up the phone, and called Sven (who, may I say, has never ever called me names or deemed me dead to him), and I said, "Honey, the strangest thing just happened." I then told him what Elliott had said to me, thinking that he would have thought it was as cruel and inhuman as I did. Of course, my sweet and deadpan man said (always in 3 words or less), "Oh, screw him…" And then he continued as if he didn't know that I was still in shock over bad ex-boyfriend behavior. Then he said, "I'm so glad you called. We're going out to dinner tonight with Jeff and Julie, so I'll pick up the girls if you'd like." You know, everyone has their own "music to their ears," but having the man I love want to spend an evening with his friends and our kids is just that.

It just puts everything in perspective for me and makes me smile constantly.

So, now let's flash forward to years later. Whenever Sven and I talk about someone who has done something horrible, one of us just looks at the other and says, "He's dead to me!" Then we do that little private-joke-between-you-and-me kind of giggle, and move on.

This now brings me to my little story. When I had to move from the house that P.D. and I lived in, mainly because of the harassment and daily threats, I picked a home that was, yes, in the suburbs. It was not a cool urban loft or hip home with rounded doorways. But let's face it: I was by myself with no financial help from anyone. I also knew that I had traumatized my girls enough by all of the mistakes I had made in the past. So hell, the least I could do was to give them a home where they could walk to a highly-rated public elementary school (there was no way I would be able to afford private schools), ride their bikes, and play with the kids in the neighborhood.

In my mind, I was thinking block parties, Kool-Aid stands (we would donate the proceeds to UNICEF), and holiday parties where we would teach all the non-Jews in the neighborhood about all the similarities between our religions and have as many Chanukah, Christmas, and Kwanzaa parties as possible. Once again, Laura Ray had a dream.

I began my little foray into Suburbiaville/Shangri-La by baking my blueberry/raspberry bars and brownies for our 2 next-door neighbors in the cul-de-sac. It didn't matter that I hadn't even unpacked all our boxes and that our new house looked like it had been hit by a tornado. I didn't care.

It didn't really matter that the tradition is that the "old" neighbors are the ones that are supposed to bake and welcome the "new" neighbors.

I didn't care. I just lovingly placed the homemade sweets on doilies on these cool platters that I bought at the dollar store (and that, in my mind, didn't look like they were dollar-store purchases). Then I dressed my sweet, not yet hormonally raging 5- and 7-year-olds in adorable outfits, brushed out the flour and butter stuck in their pigtails from baking, and gave them each a tray to hand out, to introduce themselves to our 2 neighbors.

The neighbors to the south of us were kind and sweet and very appreciative of the modest efforts toward neighborly tradition. (Thank you, trailblazer June Cleaver. I just always looked horrible in pearls!) The girls seemed very pleased with themselves, thinking that they may be onto this Welcome Wagon in reverse thing and it's not that tough. They were so excited to go to their next home, they couldn't stand it. I had to tell them not to run because the cookies and brownies would be totally disarrayed (God forbid).

My daughters rang the doorbell of the home exactly north of us. I was standing far enough away that the 2 of them thought they were doing this huge feat by themselves. And that's when it happened.

The entire family — in this huge, 2-story, perfectly arranged home, opened the door and just stared at my kids (for what seemed like forever). The mother looked at the girls, and instead of inviting the girls into their home for hot chocolate and crumpets (once again: my sick, twisted La-

La mind), she just curtly said, "What?"

No "Hello," No "My, it's nice to meet you," No "Boy, those poodle dresses sure do look cute on you." No "How did your mommy find the time to make all those homemade goodies while she was moving?" Absolutely nothing. Just a really cold "What?"

Maggie took the lead and sweetly said, "We wanted to introduce ourselves to you. We made you these cookies and if you ever want to play with us, you can!" Mollie just moved her head up and down, like she was agreeing with her big sister (that was probably the last time that ever happened.).

The Mom looked at the girls (the Dad and the two little boys just stood there staring at them as if they were aliens with horns), took the tray from their hands, and said, "I don't think so, but thank you for the cookies."

Even though they still live next door to us, I haven't been that physically close to them since that afternoon and I was hiding in the trees. Even though their two sons were about the same age as Maggie and Mollie, I just thought that they must have known about P.D. or knew that I had married the same P.O.S. twice and were afraid that my stupidity would rub off on their precious, perfect family.

Whatever it was, I lost my dream of the perfect neighborhood. The block parties, the Chanukah/Christmas parties, the progressive dinners all went out the window.

Years later, the girls and I were at the neighborhood grocery store, and as I was buying 10 for $10 cans of green beans and corn, a man was also grabbing at the same vegetable assortment I was. I looked at him and smiled. Mollie looked at me after he left to go to the pasta and rice aisle and said, "Mommy, do you know who that was?" I said, "No, Honey, I have no idea."

She opened her big brown eyes widely and said, "Oh Mommy, that's our next-door neighbor!"

I looked at her and very flatly said, "Oh, I'm sorry, Honey. He must be dead to me."

Here is a great recipe that will be a hit for any progressive dinner. You can have the recipe and claim it as your own, because we will never be invited to one.

LIZ'S DELICIOUS CHINESE COLESLAW

1 8 oz. package of coleslaw mix (shredded cabbage)
1 package of oriental flavor ramen noodles
1 3 oz. package of slivered almonds
1 bunch green onions, sliced
2 tsp of sugar
2 tsp of apple cider
½ cup oil

1. Stir coleslaw mix and green onions together.
2. Mix the vinegar, oil, and sugar with the oriental mix from the ramen noodles.
3. Pour over coleslaw mix.
4. Finally, in non-stick skillet, heat up the almonds and broken-up ramen noodles until lightly toasted.
5. Stir almonds and ramen noodles into coleslaw and serve immediately or refrigerate.

Chapter 12

"Kids Say the Darndest Things"— Brought to a Whole New Level

I know that this is a "duh," but once you're married and have kids (and in my situation, married, divorced, married an abusive jerk, had 2 kids, divorced, and then married the love of my life) work full-time, do all the soccer Mom, Girl Scout, piano lessons, and so forth, the time that you have alone with your husband adds up to about 11-1/2 minutes each week.

Every once in a while, Sven starts to feel sorry for himself, and that is when I scramble to think of ways for us to have quality time alone, even if it's only five minutes before I pass out after putting the kids to bed.

Because of this, we started a tradition about a year ago. That was, the minute the kids went to bed, Sven would jump into our bed, I would sprint to the kitchen to get a "Skinny Cow" (only has 130 calories!), split it in half and if we decided to go wild and crazy that night, we'd actually share two and then I'd run back into bed, give him his half, turn on the television and watch the Daily Show with Jon Stewart. And if I haven't fallen asleep yet, I watch the Colbert Report afterward. Isn't it just pathetic what a couple has to do to spend just a few minutes together? I love those two television shows. I always feel as though I've got to get the news any way I can, and those two guys are hysterical. So it's a great way to watch the news, and even if you feel as though you want to cry at the dismal crap going on around us, you just have to laugh at the absurdity of it all.

Anyway, we were both tucked in very comfortably with half of a Skinny Cow in hand, and a child whose name begins with an "M" (you have two to choose from, but I thought in this particular story, this M child should remain incognito) comes walking right in. Why do kids, (especially ours) nowadays have absolutely no boundaries?

"What is the matter, Honey?," I asked, and then quickly said, "Why the heck don't you ever knock before you barge right in."

"Mommy, Daddy, I have to tell you something." (Of course she just rambles on and on, and talking so excitedly, not even pausing or hesitating to answer my question or apologizing for not even knocking) And she said, "Oh, Mom, Daddy, this is so important and I didn't want to wait until the morning to tell you what I have decided to do!."

Sven and I just looked at each other and said, "OK, it better be good. What is it, Honey?" Sven decided to start asking her his litany of wishful questions (with just a wee bit of sarcasm), "Well, have you decided to be the youngest Peace Corp volunteer ever to enlist? Have you decided to travel and perform with the USO "I know! You decided to travel with Jimmy and Rosalynn Carter and work for Habitat for Humanity?" He continued, "OK, So I give up. What do you want, a new gerbil?"

No, no, no, not our kid!

She looked at both of us in her "American Girl Doll" pajamas, chocolate still on her face from the three brownies she ate for dessert, and said, squealing, like he's really starting to annoy her, God forbid, "Stop it Daddy, I really have to tell you something very important!"

OK, so now, our curiosity is piqued.

"Mommy, Daddy, I've decided that I'm going to start shaving my pubic hairs."

With that declaration, my poor defeated Sven threw the covers over his head and slid down to the foot of the bed. All I could hear was the reincarnation of The Fly (the Vincent Price version, not the later Jeff Goldblum one) where he kept on saying in a high, very pained way, "help me, help me, help me."

I was literally speechless, which doesn't happen often. Then I said,

"Sweetie, did you think you had to tell us this news at 10:30 at night?." And in an almost pleading voice, I continued, "and please, this is something that a Daddy should never have to hear!"

I then pointed to the love of my life, who was literally a buried, big blob at the bottom of our bed. "Honey," I said to M, "Look at what you've done to this man!"

She and I looked at each other and saw this 52-year-old lump at the foot of the bed, sadly whimpering "help me," and I just thought, "What the hell have I done to this man, who I love so deeply! Look at what his life has become!"

This is a favorite recipe from a dear friend of mine that is always nice to have "in reserve" when you have children:

ELLIE'S DELICIOUS AND STRONG AMARETTO SOUR JELL-O SHOTS

1 cup Amaretto DiSaronno
(2) 3-oz packages lime Jell-O
2 cups boiling water
2 tbsp lemon juice

Bring water to a boil and remove from heat. Dissolve Jell-O in boiling water, stirring at least 3 minutes. Add lemon juice. Allow to cool a bit and then add Amaretto DiSaronno.

Pour mixture into shot glasses or small paper cups.

Let shots sit in refrigerator for at least 4 hours and enjoy them when needed!

Chapter 13

Cut Thick or Thin, Any Way You Slice It, a Salami Is a Salami Is a Salami

OK, get your head out of the gutter, this chapter is basically about a 3-foot salami and its effect on a school-aged, awkward, homely, buck-toothed Jewish kid, and how parents have the ability to completely change their children's outlook on life.

This little story starts like this:

Way back when — back in the olden days, right after the dinosaur era — there was a nice, middle-class Jewish family whose grandparents emigrated from Russia to St. Louis, Missouri. Like the majority of Eastern European Jewish immigrants who had to leave their homeland to avoid religious persecution and (unsuccessful!) genocide, Louis and Essie Roodman started with nothing, and through hard work and talent, they, along with their three sons, grew their once-small delicatessen business into an almost St. Louis landmark.

Well, that may be a little bit of an exaggeration from a proud granddaughter 40-something years later, but I don't know whether you truly understand the relationship that Jews have with food. (I'm sure that if you didn't know it before you started reading either of my books, you probably have figured it out by now!) But honestly, I realized at a very young age that just by knowing how to smoke your own salmon or whitefish or having the ability to make the finest flaky pastry for a homemade knish, you will be elevated to "rock star" status in the Jewish community.

I remember when things were crazy and busy, my Zeydah ("Grandpa" in Yiddish), uncles, and father were treated like local celebrities. Not only did they have their delicatessen, but they had a "factory" in the back of the restaurant where all the Jewish deliciousness was created. The deli was actually "kosher style" and not actually kosher. My Dad always laughingly called the process of making something "kosher" as sheer "rabbi extortion." It's not, though we as a family have never, then or now, kept kosher. In fact, Sven always laughs about how he keeps more kosher than the girls and I have ever been, even though he was raised a Southern Baptist. Even though the delicatessen closed decades ago, you can still walk into many local grocery stores in the city today and see big pickle barrels with the family name and the deli's logo. (I bet you're jealous now, aren't you?)

Everything was going swimmingly in Reform Jewish la-la land. I was in the first grade. My two older sisters, Babs and Gwendolyn, would hold my hand every day as we merrily walked back and forth to school, while Johnny was still a toddler at home. Each night, when our Dad would come home with a pound of pastrami, corned beef, or lox that he personally had smoked, and like clockwork, we would scream in stereo "Oh no, Daddy, not lox again!" Today, years later, it's damn Jewish gold at about $48/lb. (My, how true luxuries are wasted on the youth. God, I sound old!)

Who knew that this little trip down memory lane would lead to such psychological trauma that I would still be thinking about this 40 years later?! I wonder if, in medical journals, they would call it something like "PTDS" (Post Traumatic Deli Syndrome)?

Well, my PTDS began the week between Chanukah and Christmas. While everyone was frantically getting ready for all the holiday parties, our Mother decided that she'd better get all the gifts ready for our sweet teachers, the mailman, the milkman, and the garbage men. Imagine my surprise when my Dad came home with about 47 3-foot-long, kosher-style salamis with humongous red bows on them!

God forbid we should give our teachers an apple, or a little holiday candle, or a nice box of chocolate-covered cherries like every other kid in the neighborhood. Oh no, not our strange family. Not only were we supposed to give these odd-looking things to people we loved and admired, we were also supposed to walk these festive salamis to school! All I could think, in my small, 6-year-old mind, "Could life get any worse?" The salamis actually were taller than me and were about half my weight.

We all screamed, "Please, Daddy, no!" You would have thought that my parents had killed our dachshund, Ricky Ricardo. Also, you must remember that I was 6 years old and didn't weigh much more than the salami itself. And of course I was summoned to carry 5 of my own (one to each of my teachers, the lunchroom lady, and the school nurse) all the way across town.

An amazing thing happened during this ordeal. You see, my sisters and I actually cried ourselves to sleep the night before our elementary school holiday party. We were horrified, thinking about the utter humiliation we were going to have to endure when we did what we were "summoned" to do by our Daddy.

Thinking about it years later, what was really pathetic about the whole ordeal is that when we all walked to school and people walked and drove by us three Jewish little girls carrying dozens of foot-long salamis with huge red bows, I don't think they were fazed at all. I think that the entire community probably thought to themselves, "Oh, that's just the Roodman kids. They are probably bringing their lunches today."

Actually, a miracle occurred. Think of our amazement when the next morning, after the "festive salami" delivery, all three of us became semi-celebrity delicatessen "rock stars" in our own right. We were shocked, but got quite used to the winks and smiles we got as big thank yous from all our teachers, the principal, and the school secretaries. Teachers that we didn't have were actually jealous of the ones that had us in their classrooms. I think everyone was experiencing what is now commonly known as "kosher-style salami envy" (something you don't hear about every day).

I guess there is a moral to this little story. And that is, for the most part, our parents are all smarter than we give them credit for. I, of course, try to remind Maggie and Mollie of that on a daily basis, even when I'm doing the most ignorant things (like telling complete strangers my deepest, darkest secrets).

I guess they should at least be grateful that they won't ever have to carry 47 logs of 3-foot-long, kosher-style meat across town anytime soon. Unless, of course, Johnny, Babs, Gwendolyn, and I decide to open our own delicatessen to continue the family tradition.

One of our all-time favorite recipes containing, of course, salami.... What did you think, that I would use a recipe with bologna or pastrami?

MATZOH AND EGGS with FRIED SALAMI

2 tbsp butter
12 eggs
½ cup milk or half-and-half
salt & pepper to taste
5 sheets of salted matzoh – slightly dampened with warm water.
1 cup of thinly sliced, kosher or kosher-style salami

Take a large skillet and fry the salami in 1 tbsp of butter until it is slightly brown on each side. Remove the salami and clean the skillet to use for the eggs.
Beat the eggs, milk, and salt and pepper together and then crunch up the slightly damp matzoh and drop it into the egg mixture. Stir it up so that all the matzoh is egg covered.
In the large skillet, melt the other tbsp of butter and pour the egg-matzoh mixture In pan. Stir constantly so that it's evenly cooked. When the eggs are almost done to your liking, gently fold the salami into the eggs and stir.
Serve immediately. Our family always loves to eat this delicacy with sour cream and strawberry jelly. What you eat it with is up to you. But try it; it's delicious!

Chapter 14

Sometimes Being a Serial People-Pleaser Can Be a Problem

Why is it whenever I start to write a chapter, Sven sits down close to me on the green couch and hopefully says, "Honey, you're not going to write about what just happened, are you?" The answer, this time, is no. I'm now going to write about what happened a few months ago. So, if you try, you can probably hear Sven's sigh of relief.

When my first book came out, I received several requests to speak with other local authors. The one that is the subject of this chapter was called "The Local Authors Shoot-Out." Sounds pretty violent for an affair at a library, don't you think?

Well, I was flattered when asked to speak in front of (I hoped) hundreds, or maybe even thousands (we all can dream, right?) of readers and new fans. I couldn't wait to meet other struggling authors. I've always thought that we all need to help each other, for it's definitely not a competition. This writing business is not an easy one to break into!

A college friend of Sven's, who is now a very successful agent in the New York publishing world, told me she was very sorry, but unless her partners could see the next Harry Potter or 50 Shades of Grey series (sorry guys, no whips and chains and submissive stuff in my book. I was married to Psycho Dick twice for way too long, so that's all you're going to get of sadomasochism), complete with an option for the possible Hollywood motion picture, no one wants to take a chance on a first-time writer.

Going back to my sad, somewhat masochistic story (watch out, E.L James, you may just have some competition after all), the day of this big library event coincided with our city's St. Patrick's Day Parade. This is where tens of thousands of people (whether Irish or just Irish for the day) line up and wait hours to watch the floats (some of them featured the month before in the second largest Mardi Gras festival in the country, but painted green).

Have you ever heard the old saying, "the difference between men and boys is the price of their toys"? Well, that saying is very true, and it pertains to Sven and a group of his very close friends. Together for over 20 years, this group of about 25 guys have named themselves the "Mystic Knights of The Purple Haze" (Jimi Hendrix being their patron saint). These guys (and several devoted and talented women) design, build, and execute a Mardi Gras float that for over the past 25 years has, with impressive regularity, won 1st place out of hundreds of other floats. Sven is the DJ-emcee of the krewe (which really means that he gets to ride on the float, emphasize the beauty and brilliance of his krewe, chat up the huge crowds and play funky New Orleans music), while everyone else walks miles, including his wife. I throw beads and moon pies while I try to pretend that I'm cool and can dance at the same time.

Anyway, because the MKPH float won 1st Place (once again), they were invited to be in the prestigious St. Patrick's Day parade. It is always the "family-friendly" parade versus the "not-so-family-friendly" Mardi Gras parade, and gives the entire crew permission to bring their kids along to ride on the float. (Or, as Sven likes to tell the Mardi Gras crowd, "We're putting the carnal back in carnival!)

Being the "queen of multitaskers," I planned ahead and told Sven that I could do it all, even though both of these monumental affairs ran back to back. I went on a baking and cooking frenzy. Maggie, Mollie, and I made hundreds of cookies, brownies, and blueberry bars for the krewe and their kids, and then I cleaned up the kitchen to start cooking again for the library event.

Don't ask me why I always spend more money on these events than I end up making by selling my books. I'm sure it stems from my huge need to make sure everyone likes me, my books, and my severe condition of Generosity Tourettes. But for God's sake, does Paula Deen or Rachael Ray feel the need to cook every recipe at every book signing they do? I don't think so. Admittedly, they are much smarter and more business savvy than me! If we ever meet, maybe you'll be able to explain this huge, stupid flaw of mine. I promise to be very appreciative and will gladly give you my $20 co-pay.

So, I was up until about 3 a.m., cooking, cleaning and preparing for the big day. That morning, Sven and I gathered up our kids, their friends, the dozen trays of food that I had prepared, hundreds of books that I thought I'd sell, fuchsia table cloths, doilies galore, etc. I also thought ahead of time and suggested that we had better take two cars just in case I had to leave early from the parade. With all the crap we had, it actually took two cars (a Mayflower moving van would have helped) to transport everything. You'd have thought that we were driving cross-country for a month-long "Feed the Hungry" (on butter and sugar) tour.

After we set up the library event, we drove downtown, parked my car at the end of the parade route, took Sven's car to the area where the parade was to begin, and then began to get ready for the huge parade.

I was costumed as a diner waitress from the 50s, with a five-foot beehive hairdo and a cute little waitress dress and apron. It was cute but very top heavy, and I've never been the most coordinated person around, so it was a lot of effort just to balance myself and stay standing.

The girls and I were handing out all our delicious baked goods for the hard-working krewe and their families. The 16-year-old niece of one of the guys was standing on top of the float. I had met her before. She was an adorable, sweet girl with Down syndrome, and I know she had no idea of her strength and her ability to throw objects. But, I think she was dispensing fruit that other people from the krewe had decided to bring (unlike all the unhealthy and fattening stuff that I brought) in a way that she thought would be more time efficient than just handing it out in person. So, she threw a huge naval orange to me, with force and speed that would make a major league baseball pitcher very proud. The only problem was, it hit me in my eye so hard that not only did I and my five-foot beehive fall straight to the ground, I passed out for a few minutes. When I finally got up, I found out that I had a huge black and purple eye to take to my next speaking engagement.

About 8 minutes later, when I finally woke up from my slight concussion and realized that our float was to be 168th out of 172 floats, I knew that the only way that I would make it to the library on time was if I left my family and the krewe members, ran down the parade route 3 miles downtown, and got to my car (which hopefully I could still drive, even with my concussion and swollen eye). I remember seeing (with my good eye) parade watchers pointing at me and probably saying, "Look at that pathetic thing!" and "Mommy, Daddy, that lady must have really wanted to be in the parade. What do you think happened to her?!"

I finally found my car, talked a police officer into letting me drive out of the barricaded street (looking back now, he probably thought I was driving myself to the emergency room), and quickly drove about 5 miles to the library.

When I got to the library, I ran to the bathroom, changed out of my goofy waitress outfit, put on some normal clothes, took off the wig (which had left an indentation the size of a smaller version of the Grand Canyon on my forehead), and quietly walked into the event that had already begun.

Three seconds after I sat down at my already-prepared table, my name was called to speak in front of the very serious, urban, primarily African American audience. They were all there to hear readings from "poetry slam" participants, whose titles seemed to have themes that could be summed up as, "Why I resent the hell out of all white people 7 days a week"

So, now you have the entire picture. Here I was, some stupid bleached blonde from the suburbs who had been up all night, with a black eye, indentation on my head, uncontrollably shaking (probably the effects of the concussion and the realization that I totally screwed up by agreeing to speak at this engagement where I clearly didn't belong). Very politely, I began reading by first asking everyone if they'd like to try one of my blueberry bars. They all, of course, looked at me as if I were an alien. I read my little chapter (about "Mollie and the Beef") and then quickly sat down at my table.

I can't even explain how relieved I was that my part of this event was over. I was breathing that huge sigh of relief when a bald man with a 99.9-percent tattooed head and 23 ear piercings on his left ear alone, whose table was right next to me, leaned over to whisper something to me – of course not wanting to interrupt the author who was speaking after me. I leaned to hear him, thinking that he was going to say, "great job" or something like, "I read your book and I loved it." But, as God is my witness, he said as softly as he could (even though the entire room could hear), "YOU SUCKED!"

I had no response. I could feel a tear fall from my bad eye (not knowing if it was from his kind critique or just the aftermath from the eight pound orange). And I just looked at him and said, very feebly, in a stupidly sweet voice, "Well, I'm sorry that you feel that way."

At that very moment, Sven and the girls tramped in, covered with all their green regalia. They whistled, hooted and hollered for me (even though they missed my sucky performance). And Sven looked at me and saw how pathetic I was and could tell that I was ready to just let loose and do the "ugly cry." So he just walked up to me, grabbed my hand and said, "OK, Honey, let's get out of here and get something to eat. We'll clean this mess up later."

I really couldn't wait to leave. With both my head and ego bruised, I held my husband's hand and walked out. On a side note, the tattooed man, who I'll just call from now on "Urban-Sluggo" or "Cityfied Bazooka Joe," e-mailed several days later and said that he had just finished my book and thought it was funny. I wonder what he'll say after he reads this chapter?

The next morning, I woke up thinking (and hoping) that maybe the day before was all just a really bad dream, until, of course, I felt the huge, sore lump on my head and saw my very black and purple eye. I turned to Sven, who was waking up at the same time, and quietly said, "Honey, do you believe how horribly yesterday went?" Of course, my husband of few, but perfectly "on point" words, stared right into my black eye and disfigured head and blandly said, "Hon, it's always helpful to know who your target audience is."

I knew that this chapter called for a recipe that was "orange" in honor of what hit me in the head, and for decades, our Grandma Essie brought this cake to our house every Sunday for dinner. It's delicious, and I just wanted to make sure that whatever orange recipe I chose would be soft, just in case it gets thrown!

GRANDMA ESSIE'S DELICIOUS ORANGE SUNSHINE BUNDT CAKE

2 cups all-purpose flour
1-1/2 cups sugar
2 tbsp baking powder
7 eggs, separated
¼ tsp salt
¼ cup orange juice
½ cup vegetable oil
¼ cup water
2 tsp vanilla extract
1 tbsp grated orange peel
2 tsp grated lemon peel
½ tsp cream of tartar

ICING:
½ cup of powdered sugar
2 tbsp solid shortening
1 tbsp butter, softened
1 8-oz can of crushed pineapple, drained completely

Directions
Sift the flour, sugar, baking powder and salt into a large bowl. Make a well in the center. In another bowl, beat egg yolks until thickened and lemon colored. Beat in the orange juice, oil, water, vanilla, and orange and lemon peels. Pour into the well in the dry ingredients. Beat with a wooden spoon until smooth. In a mixing bowl, beat egg whites on medium speed until foamy. Add cream of tartar. Beat until stiff peaks form. Gradually fold into batter.
Transfer to an ungreased 10-inch tube pan. Bake at 325 degrees for 55-60 minutes or until cake springs back when lightly touched. Immediately invert cake; cool completely. Loosen cake from sides of pan. Remove cake and place on a serving platter.

Icing
Blend powdered sugar, shortening and butter until smooth. Fold in pineapple and sugar and shortening and until smooth. Spread over top of cake. Spoon pineapple over icing and enjoy.
When I go wild and crazy, I like to add coconut and chopped pecans to the icing.

CHAPTER 15

A Subliminally Repressed Birthday Party

By now, I hope that you – my new BFF — have related to some of my stories. Or then again, you're probably screaming a loud resounding "No way have I done all the stupid things you've done in your life!" But please be honest: there has to be at least one or two stupid things that I have done that you can relate to. If not, that is perfectly fine; but please, if we ever meet in person, just let me continue to live in my little bubble and allow me to think that everyone else's life is as insane as mine. And let's face it, we are all "women of the millennium" who have taken multi-tasking to a whole new level. And how the heck are we supposed to be perfect in everything? So today, that's my "shtick," and I'm shticking to it.

Every once in a while, I'll wake up from a dream about something that happened in my past. I guess because it was something that I had repressed for years, the dream thing is how my mind is trying to purge these memories. That's what happened to me this morning when I woke up in a cold, sticky sweat and thought I'd better quickly write down what happened over 20 years ago, so that my mind doesn't repress it again. And who knows when it will appear again? I'll probably be dead by then.

It all happened one hot, humid day in Midwest Suburbiaville, when my family decided to plan a surprise 24th birthday party for me. It was during a time in my life where I thought that I had arrived, I had a good job that paid more money than I ever thought I was worth. I had just bought a home and car by myself, probably at retail, because I refused to allow my father to help me with the negotiating, and because of my horrendous Generosity Tourettes (I even had it in my 20s!). God forbid I bargain for the best price. (But that will be another repressed dream to come, I'm sure). Also, I had recently broken up with my first real boyfriend.

Since I was so very mature at this time, I thought that my time for wild and crazy dating times had finally arrived. There was only one slight problem with my plan. Thinking back, and with a brief bit of therapy behind me, I was actually so hurt by my first real break-up, I must have thought that I couldn't handle another relationship.

I must have also thought that if I consumed mass quantities of Nacho Cheese Doritos and Peanut M&Ms, I would have gained enough weight (about 68 lbs to be exact, but who's counting?) that no man in his right mind would ever ask me out.

Well, my experiment worked perfectly. I don't think I had a date for at least two years after that. Then one of my closest friends took my hand, and all she had to say was, "OK, Lou, I want to start working out with you six days a week, and let's help each other to get back into shape" (she was in perfect, size 4 shape at the time, but was sweet enough to include herself as "part of the plan").

Anyway, here I was, at a whopping 206 lbs, and wasn't even thinking of my birthday. In fact, I was trying everything in my power to forget that the day was even arriving. My family had this lovely plan to throw a surprise party for me. There was just one teeny, tiny problem. My sisters and brother – even though we've always been very close — had no idea who the heck they should invite.

They had a little family pow-wow, and together they decided to ask another close friend of mine (who had access to my brand new, tiny, green, $47,000 house) to retrieve my address book. Suzi took on the job, and of course unbeknownst to me, sneaked into my sparsely furnished home (with the small exception of 6 bags of Doritos and M&Ms) and took from the wall my James Taylor Mud Slide Slim calendar that had all my phone numbers scribbled all over the pages.

Words like "shock" and "horror" would have been an understatement when I walked into my parents' home on the humid Saturday night in

August to see not only my few very loyal friends, cousins and family members at this party, but also the creepy exterminator I hired once when I had ants in the kitchen. This was a guy who I dated once and who started to stalk me. Also present was the strange couple that had sold me my green house. Then, my favorite horrifying memory is when I looked at my parents' old leather couch and saw this creep (who brought his wife, of course) who sold me his car, and who was in the process of suing me in small claims court for not paying him the $100 more that he thought his used car was worth!

I truly didn't know if I should laugh, cry or puke in the middle of this party given in my honor. Here I was, standing in my three-quarter-zipped, black stirrup pants. What the heck are you supposed to say to some strange guy who is suing you? "Well hello, Bill, would you like a piece of birthday cake? And by the way, the reason why I never paid you the last $100 was your car broke down three times and the muffler fell off in the middle of the highway."

To be totally honest, the rest of the night was a complete blur. I have no idea what happened. I don't know if anyone actually had a good time, what kind of food and drinks with umbrellas were served (which is usually what I focus on the most). I truly repressed the entire three hours and 18 minutes.

I'm sure this chapter would have been longer, but I'm betting there are things I still am choosing not to remember. If you'd like any more details of this total fiasco, which basically represents how I had lost control of my youth, and the frame of mind (and body) I was in when I first met Psycho Dick (only about 2 months later), I guess you'll have to wait until I have another dream like I did last night. Who knows, it may just "un-repress" details of the rest of the night, in which case I promise to write a chapter in my next book to tell you the rest of the sordid details.

Is there a hypnotist in the house?

This easy and delicious recipe may have been served that night. I just can't remember.

JOANNA'S UNBELIEVABLY DELICIOUS, TOO-EASY-TO-BELIEVE SPANISH CHEESECAKE SOPAPILLA
(Trust me on this one.)

Preheat oven to 350 degrees

2 packages of crescent rolls

3 8-oz packages of cream cheese (Joanna uses 1/3 fat cream cheese)

1-1/2 cups sugar

1 tsp vanilla

1 stick of melted butter

½ cup sugar

1 tsp cinnamon (or to taste)

Use 1 package of the crescent rolls to completely line the bottom of an ungreased 9x13 pan.

Blend cream cheese, sugar and vanilla until creamy.

Spread mixture on the crescent rolls.

Cover with second package of crescent rolls.

Pour butter, sugar and cinnamon mixture on top and spread evenly.

Bake at 350 for 45 minutes or until golden brown.

Let cool a little before serving.

For a change, if you'd like, I also put a layer of thinly sliced, peeled apples on top of the cream cheese mixture. Or a can of drained crushed pineapple is delicious as well!

Enjoy! And let me know how many times you make this one in a 1-month period!

Chapter 16

One Typical Day in the Life...

Imagine Sven's surprise one beautiful Fall Sunday morning, when he opened the downstairs bathroom and saw me sitting on the floor typing away. He gave me a knowing, sympathetic, and somewhat "Oh, you sad little thing" kind of look when he realized that I wanted to quickly write down a chapter before I forgot the subject and then wouldn't remember it until months later, even if you paid me thousands and thousands of dollars.

I choose this little oasis of a hideaway (just saying this is almost as pathetic as it gets), because

#1 – This particular bathroom isn't used very often, so it's kept somewhat clean.

#2 – It has a lock on the door that the kids are unable to jiggle to get in.

#3 – It's fairly soundproof, so I can't hear the kids screaming at each other or the dogs fighting.

#4 – I'm far enough away not to be reminded that the refrigerator needs emptying and the laundry room has four days' worth of dirty clothes that are starting to smell.

#5 – I'm far enough away from the little bit of puppy puke that I'm waiting for the girls — who swore on their lives that if Sven and I allowed them to have a new "rescue Chihuahua" (doesn't that sound like the quintessential oxymoron?) to clean up. And I know that if I see it or smell it, I'll cave in and clean it myself. (These life lessons can just be so damn difficult on the parents, don't you agree?)

#6 – I'm away from my office, and being there will just remind me that I have four reports that I am late sending to my boss about my performance review. (Now, if that's not the most perfect way to spend a Sunday morning, then, nothing is.) But the biggest reason for me to lock myself in the downstairs bathroom and sit on the floor to type is (drum roll, please) ...

#7 – It's the only bathroom in the house that has carpet on the floor and wouldn't be cold to sit on.

Oh, these little things in life always mean so much! This brings me to my story, which will probably resonate across the country. It is one that every woman will read and have an "a-ha" moment — but not in a good way.

Yesterday, I was trying to straighten up the garage. Basically, I wanted to do this because it's fall – soon to be winter, and it would be nice to have room in our two-car garage to park at least one of our cars in it during the ice, snow and sleet season. What a concept! Well, the Ray family (and I know that we're not alone with this one) always have so much crap in our garage, it's tough to make room for those little things such as your used, but still somewhat expensive, wanting-to-keep-for-the-next-10 years-or until-it-dies automobile.

As I was huffing and puffing, cleaning and getting rid of a ton of stuff I hadn't seen in years, I ran across a 10-gallon bag of stuffed animals that were all smooshed together.

My entire body immediately started to shake wildly. It was as if these memories that I had repressed for over 11 years had finally been exorcised, and my body reacted in the most unflattering way. Why, you may ask, would my body go through such an ordeal over a big bag of teddy bears, Barneys, thousands of dollars' worth of Build-A-Bears (what a smart racket that is!) and ugly and creepy Telletubby dolls that were so popular in the late 90s (until Jerry Falwell declared the purple one gay! One of America's low points in history, if you ask me)?

Well, I'll tell you. I had to seal up all of these creatures, along with all my sheets, covers, bedspreads, pillows, and everything else I owned because the daycare that the kids were in at the time (they were around

3 and 5) had to close, owing to an epidemic of lice. It started with a sweet little girl who will be etched in my memory forever as "Typhoid Mackenzie." She had beautiful, very long hair. And unbeknownst to all the kids, the teachers, and my friendly, "let's crawl all over you and play with you" Maggie and Mollie, had passed along these disgusting creatures to everyone at the entire school.

I am so ignorant to so many things in life, and this was definitely one of them. I really had never even heard of them. So, I was washing the kids' hair in the bathtub one night and saw some rough patches on their heads. I just did the thing I did so well, which was to call the pediatrician and make an appointment to see why both of their heads had these strange-looking circles on them?

So you can imagine my surprise the next day, when the young pediatrician quickly "threw" us into quarantine as if I and my sweet little girls — dressed in, of course, their finest faux leopard sweat suits with matching faux leopard bows — were horrible social pariahs! By the way, this story is making me itch all over, just thinking about it. All of a sudden, the strange-looking circles on their heads quickly became swarms of lice flying and jumping from head to head. I started screaming, the kids started crying, and the doctor quickly wrote me a prescription for Nix. I realized, hours later, that a prescription wasn't necessary at all when the Walgreens pharmacist just pathetically laughed at me when I handed him the scrip. He just pointed to the "lice aisle." Who would have known that they had an entire aisle for those disgusting creatures! My doctor was just giving me the "prescription" so that I (who ended up having a few crawling on me as well), along with my two precious daughters, would get the hell out of her office!

Looking back now, I do have to say that I may have over-reacted just a bit. It may have been because I was #1 - on the tail end of the Psycho Dick marriage (for the second time), and #2, everything seemed like it was just spinning out of control and I was trying to keep it all together for the girls. Not wanting them to know that I was falling apart, trying to keep my new, high-pressured job and figure out how to pay the bills when I realized that P.D.'s eighth job in three years wasn't paying a darn thing.

In the midst of all of this fun, I was charging adorable outfits for the girls right and left on my Macy's card (the only credit card that had anything left on it to charge on) to get ready for a trip to Denver, Colorado to celebrate my wonderful sister Gwendolyn's two sons' Bar Mitzvah the next weekend. It was a huge family gala, and we had been planning on it forever (about 13 years, actually).

After applying this horrible, lethal-smelling stuff on my precious kids' heads and mine about 4 different times, I set out on a mission to rid ourselves of this disgusting plight. I threw away perfectly clean clothes, bedding and towels. I got rid of all of those helpless stuffed animals (they didn't see it coming) and then I drove the kids to the neighborhood hair salon. (Looking back, we all were probably a little high from the Nix fumes.) When I walked in and explained what had happened, everyone started to whisper and glare at us as if we had leprosy. The manager walked in and said, "I'm sorry Ma'am. You must leave immediately!" I started to cry, and the girls just looked at me with their big brown eyes, and I think Mollie said, "Mommy, why are they making us leave? Why don't they like us?"

I don't know why it hit me just then, but I thought, "This is it". This may have been one of the worst moments of my life.

I know it sounds like I'm being dramatic, but I'll bet, if any of you, my new BFFs, have had this happen to you (and I wouldn't wish it on my worst enemy), you totally understand. I would definitely put it in the "worst moment" category, right underneath my father passing away, or when I realized that P.D. had pretended to go to work for months and was really sitting at a bar from 8:00 a.m. to 5:00 p.m. every day, flirting (and who knows what else, yet again, who cares?) with a girl by the name of Debbie.

I drove away feeling totally humiliated and ended up driving aimlessly, not knowing where to go or what to do. I was totally lost trying to figure out how to solve this horrible problem. Out of the blue, I somehow (it must have been what the experts call a "head lice epiphany") remembered reading that African Americans are immune to head lice because of some products they use in their hair. So, I quickly got the heck out of the snobby county and my car drove itself into the city. I then found the nearest urban salon and walked in with my two traumatized kids, who couldn't figure out why Mommy was shaking and crying, and the people there were so unbelievably sweet.

Three separate hair stylists quickly put all three of us in chairs, and they quickly cut all our hair in very cute bobs, if I do say so myself. Then they swept away all our hair, with all of those gross bugs, and we were done with it. Looking back, the saddest aftermath of the entire ordeal was that the beautiful curls that Maggie and Mollie had never grew back. Both of them now have hair that is bone straight. Oh well.

Things were finally getting back to as normal as it got in the dysfunctional P.D. family. I was scurrying around, trying to figure out how I could afford to put even more on my Macy's charge to buy new linens, towels, and everything else I had thrown away. I also packed three separate suitcases, figuring out all of the weekend's outfits for the beautiful Bar Mitzvah extravaganza weekend. According to P.D, he had to fly to Denver by himself on a later plane because of his job. I didn't argue with him at all. I was actually relieved that we were going to be on a plane without him. You know, when you think that the worst is over, and that nothing else could go wrong, all you can say is 'never mind'.

Well, that Friday morning at 6:45 a.m. (and we had to get to the airport at around 5:00 a.m.), we finally got on the plane. (To add further insult to injury, I later found out that they had lost all our luggage and wouldn't be able to deliver it until late Saturday afternoon.)

To the day that I die, I'll never forget this moment. We were on the same plane with most of my family. The girls and I were lucky enough to sit in the sixth row next to each other and they were all situated with their Juicy Juices and granola bars, crayons, dolls, yadda yadda yadda. My sister Babs and her family were sitting in a few of the very back rows. The stewardess was giving her shpiel, pointing to the exit doors and showing how to use one of those fake seat belts, and I was just sitting there, sighing to myself, slightly smiling, like "OK, Lou, you did it. You got through this chapter in your life mostly unscathed. The rest of weekend is going to be just fabulous!"

That was the shortest moment of self-satisfaction I've ever had. All of a sudden, as the plane was completely quiet, my 10-year-old niece screamed from the 27th row, "Hey Aunt Lou, Do the girls still have head lice?" The entire plane gave a simultaneous, in stereo surround sound, loud "eeeeeeeeeekkkk"! If I could have crawled under the seat of the plane, I would have. I just knew that I wouldn't have fit.

As a recipe side-note to this story, I was reading this to my best friend Helga. I asked her if she thought I should just skip the recipe for this story, because just thinking about a recipe that goes with this particular subject is just completely, utterly disgusting.

She said, "Lou, you need to do something comforting…because that's just what you needed when all of this was happening."

I just thought it was funny as to what she thought was comforting, and what I thought was comforting…so, I'll just give you both recipes. Can you see the slight difference between her and me?!?

Her Comforting Recipe:
HELGIE'S STRAIGHT UP

1 cup of Grey Goose Vodka
1/2 cup triple sec
1/2 cup cranberry juice
1/4 cup freshly squeezed lime juice

Directions:
Pour all ingredients into a cocktail shaker with ice. Shake well and pour through a strainer into four martini glasses.

Her Comforting Recipe:
GWENDOLYN'S DELICIOUS HOME-MADE & EASY CHICKEN POT PIE

1 package of pillsbury pie crust (contains 2 crusts for both top and bottom)
1 lb. of skinless, boneless chicken breast halves – cubed
1 cup of sliced carrots
½ cup sliced celery
1 cup frozen green peas
1/3 cup chopped onion
1/3 cup of butter
2 large 30 oz. jars of chicken gravy
½ teaspoon of salt
¼ teaspoon of black pepper

Preheat Oven to 425 degrees.
Place bottom pie crust in deep dish 9-inch pie pan. Seal edges and make several small slits in the bottom of pan. Bake for 10 minutes until golden brown and then set aside.
In a large saucepan, melt butter and sauté chicken for several minutes.
Add onions, carrots, celery, peas, salt and pepper for several additional minutes.
Add the 2 jars of chicken gravy and allow mixture to simmer.
Pour hot mixture carefully into the pie pan.
Cover the pie with the second unbaked pie crust.
Seal edges and make several small slits in the top to allow steam to escape.
Bake in preheated oven for 30 to 35 minutes, or until pastry is golden brown and filling is bubbly.
Cool for 10 minutes before serving.

CHAPTER 17

Face It:
Sometimes the Truth Just Hurts

Maybe you remember reading a chapter in my first book where I told you how much more painful it was for me to divorce one of my best friends than it was when I divorced P.D.? I rambled on about the small faction of women who are incapable of having girlfriends, and then wrote that the vast majority of those women in the world at some point in time had dated my husband Sven.

When my dose of FGK (Finally Good Karma) hit me and I met him, we were both in our 40s. So, I'd be a fool to think that his list of exes was not a long one. I just never imagined that it was the size of the Mississippi River! I also would have been a fool to exclude all these women from our lives after we married. Some of them are absolutely wonderful ladies who I have grown to really like. I couldn't even begin to tell you how many of Sven's ex-girlfriends have become very close friends. They have been to our house for numerous lunches and dinners, babysat our kids, served as our Buddhist gardener, etc. But the one that I wouldn't allow to step fifty feet from our home is the subject of this chapter.

I'm sure that each one of you (and your significant other) has that "one person" – it may be yours, and then again, it's most probably your boyfriend's or husband's ex-lover. It's the person who, when their name is brought up, you can just see on your partner's face, that teeny tiny twitch or twinge of pain. That's what always happens when this "one

Lou's in the News Cheesy Shrimp Grits - Chapter 1

Pammy's Four Layer Baked Alaska - Chapter 2

Tinkerbell's Famous Cherries Jubilee - Chapter 3

Patti's Spinach Squares - Chapter 4

Crab Strudel a la Lou – Chapter 5

Spinach Strudel a la Boo – Chapter 6

Sistah Wendy's Cherry Cheese Strudel - Chapter 7

Homemade Guacamole Made by Someone Who Has No Time - Chapter 8

Dr. Alex's Espresso Bean Chocolate Fudgy Cupcakes - Chapter 9

Hollywood's Cheeseball a la Schmoo - Chapter 10

Liz's Delicious Chinese Coleslaw - Chapter 11

Ellie's Strong and Delicious Amaretto Jell-O Shots - Chapter 12

Matzoh Eggs with Fried Salami - Chapter 13

Grandma Essie's Orange Sunshine Cake - Chapter 14

Joanna's Unbelievably Delicious, Too Easy to Believe Spanish Cheesecake Sopapilla - Chapter 15

Gwendolyn's Homemade Chicken Pot Pie - Chapter 16

Dajon's Delicious Shrimp Dijon - Chapter 17

Kathy's Infamous Jell-O Pudding Shots - Chapter 18

The Best Dad in the World's Favorite Chopped Chicken Salad - Chapter 19

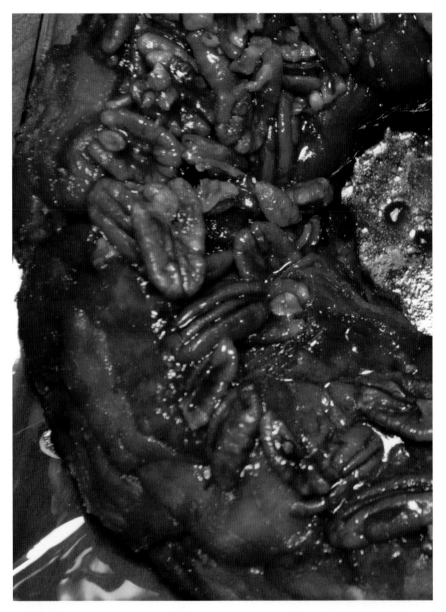

Sharon's Sticky Monkey Bread – Chapter 20

Taylor's Guilt Ridden Nutty Sticky Balls - Chapter 21

Davey's Favorite Caesar Salad with Grilled Shrimp - Chapter 22

Brother David's Jamaican Snapper - Chapter 23

Shirley's Delicious Swirly Noodle Macaroni & Cheese - Chapter 24

The Second Best Matzoh Ball Soup Ever – Chapter 25

Kathy's Bunko Drunko Slusho - Chapter 26

person's" name is mentioned.

I have come to accept this, and it's taken me only ten years. I guess I'm in that remedial class of old lovers. And though I know deep down in my heart and soul that Sven's and my relationship is everlasting (from my mouth to God's ear!), she is the one person that I am still a little jealous over. I'm not proud of it, but at least I can admit it to my best friends.

Well, I will call that person Angelica. (And, by the way, I'm naming her after the bitchy little Rugrat that you prayed your little girl would not turn into, not Ms. Huston, who I think is fabulous). Anway, Angelica was Sven's on-and-off girlfriend for over a year. They even lived together for about two months before I think he realized that having knock-down drag-out fights over the disorganization of his sock drawer was not the way he wanted to spend the rest of his life.

Angelica is a pretty, blonde psychologist. I did think it was a bit odd that the one ex who really got under his skin was a psychologist, just like Elliot, the neurotic psychiatrist that I dated for over a year before I met Sven. He was the one whose family knew me as the big "Farmer Jew." Even though I knew he was an absolute nut job, I must admit that he was a tough one to shake. I'm thinking there has to be a mandatory class that all psychologists and psychiatrists must take, called "Mind Games with Your Lover 101."

Let me also add that, true to my theory, Angelica doesn't have any close girlfriends at all. She's also had more boyfriends in her lifetime than Carter's had pills (God, that's an oldie) — or should I say, "more than Kardashian women have boob jobs." She dated a lot of these men at the same time. I guess you could say she was a practiced [boyfriend] multi-tasker.

Like the fool that I am, I thought there really were no women that I couldn't befriend, especially someone who my husband had loved in the past. I was under the illogical assumption that if he could find enough things to love about her, I certainly could. So, imagine my surprise when I finally met her.

Months after Sven and I got married, she surprised us by showing up at a concert he was emceeing. When I first saw her staring at me from across the bar, I (being the naive dipshit that I am) got up from the table and introduced myself to her. I told her that I had heard sweet things about her. (Of course I left out the fact of her being a big fat cheater and also the little story about her having a huge hang-up about unorganized sock drawers.)

Well, she totally caught me off guard. Here I was, ready to not like her at all, and all of a sudden I started to feel sorry for the girl. (See, I told you that they are good!). She told me how her life was in total disarray, that she was depressed, and that she didn't think she'd ever find the happiness that I had.

Oh, my God. I felt so bad for my new soul sister! I did what I do so damn naturally, and that was to invite her to come to our home for dinner. I then G.T. (aka: my made-up disease, Generosity Tourettes) spewed that I was going to try to fix her up with some single attorney or neighbor that I knew. I was even thinking about what I was going to make for dinner and what the kids would wear the night she came over. She was tearing up and sniveling, we were hugging and I thought, "I was so wrong thinking that she was the enemy. She could easily become one of my new best friends. Would miracles never cease?!

All during my deep, intimate conversation with Angelica, Sven was looking at us, and his facial expression clearly screamed, "Am I in Hell?!" He had this look on his face like he had just seen a poltergeist hovering over his wife, and I know he was thinking, "Oh, my God — it's not going to be pretty when we get home!" I just gave him "that look," trying to comfort him and to let him know, "Don't worry, Honey. I totally understand now. It's OK; I've got everything covered."

So, of course, after she and I talked, I had to pee (because that's just what I do every ten to fifteen minutes) and went to the dinky little restroom at the bar that had shower curtains as doors for the stalls. When I got out, imagine my surprise when my new BFF was sitting with Sven – I hadn't realized what a "close talker" she was. She was holding his hand and patting it in a way that you would pet your puppy, and in her soft, fake, (and disgusting) Betty Boop voice, I could hear her saying, "Oh Sven, are you really happy with her? It doesn't look like you are. Don't worry; you can tell me the truth."

I was shocked that someone who had just poured her heart out to me and who I had just invited to a nice tenderloin dinner (which I had already planned in my head, and we would have two different accompanying sauces, a béarnaise and a peppercorn with sautéed mushrooms), was trying to pick up my husband! What the hell was that? She must not be the new best friend that I thought she'd be after talking to her for an entire eight minutes! Just writing this makes me feel even dumber than I felt at that moment!

Sven quickly took her hand off of his, gave me a look like, "What the heck am I supposed to do, Honey?" and walked up on stage to dedicate a sweet Van Morrison song to me. His only punishment for having such bad taste in girlfriends (like I should even begin to talk!), is that he's had to endure listening to me bring her up on a semi-monthly basis, usually saying things like, "I can't believe women like that really exist." I think he finds it a little amusing. I must admit that I'm still a little jealous over this woman, but now that I know what she's really like, the jealousy has dissipated quite a bit.

Fast forward to 6 years later.

Sven decided to throw himself a little "birthday concert." He couldn't think of anything he would enjoy more than to hire his favorite musicians and friends to play with him for a few hours at this nice bar/restaurant/ delicatessen that has quite a following.

The restaurant, which is right down the street from the eclectic bar that had the art gallery that displayed the artist's P.P. (Penis Period) that was the subject of Chapter 6, is rather small, so what many patrons do is order their excellent sandwiches and then set up tables and chairs outside the place, all along this urban, fun street, to hear the music.

Happily, there ended up being hundreds of people just showing up to dance, jam, and party all night with the birthday boy. Of course I felt as though I needed to be the hostess for the event celebrating my dear Sven. But since it was at a different venue from our home, the only thing that I could think of doing was to order the biggest birthday cake I could find and put a picture of my handsome hubby on it. After the second set of music, after we sang Happy Birthday with a "bluesy" feel, I ran around the restaurant and then around the neighborhood handing out hundreds of pieces of birthday cake.

Imagine how I felt, sweaty, icing all over my clothes (and probably my face, hands, and feet) when I ended up handing out one of the last pieces of cake to a perfectly coiffed, beautifully outfitted Angelica! She was standing at the back of the room, just staring at Sven with her cow eyes. She looked me up and down, almost pityingly, and said, "Sorry, I don't eat cake," and then just kept staring at my clueless husband.

Almost in a robot-like fashion, I picked up my 15-lb purse (it too, covered with cake), got into my car, and drove home with tears streaming down my face. I just hated how she made me feel. I think I was angrier with myself than I was with her. But I think what really drove me to my pitiful "ugly cry" was just the fact that there really are women out there who feel no guilt at all flirting with other women's husbands. It just irks me no end. I guess I just did the only thing I know how to do (and quite well, if I do say so myself), and that was to just leave and cry for about 15.2 miles down the highway.

When Sven got home, leaving his own party a little early to try to find me, he looked at me as if I had lost my mind and said, "Doll, why the hell did you leave so early?" He continued, sounding a little agitated and perplexed. "All of a sudden, I looked around and you weren't there! I thought maybe you were just in the kitchen cleaning up the huge cake mess, and then Tom told me that you had left, and he thought he saw you crying. What the heck happened?"

I always think that he knows me so well, and then at other times I realize that it's not his fault that he's a man and somewhat clueless. So, I took a big breath, gathered my wits, and said, in a "wounded puppy" sort of nasally voice (trust me, my voice couldn't be sexy even if I tried, and with snot and tears running down my face, I was even more pathetic!), "I can't believe you invited Angelica to your birthday party!" He looked at me as if I were nuts and said, "Hon, I didn't invite anybody! She must have seen one of the posters that were up advertising it all over town and decided to come. I couldn't block her from coming into a public place, could I?!"

He continued, "I don't know why she still bothers you, Babe — you've got the papers and the man, true?" Then he said, "She's just a party girl, and she found out that there was a free party to go to!" As I wiped the snot off my face and understood what he was trying to say, I realized that I may have had my feelings hurt for no damn reason at all, except for my own stupid insecurities. I decided to go completely off subject. I blew my nose and said, "Well, Honey, do you think I'm a 'party girl'?" Sven just looked at me, and in his deadpan, right-on voice, he said, "Oh, Hon, you're not a PARTY GIRL, you're a DINNER PARTY girl!"

Once again, my husband hit it out of the ballpark.

This recipe is a dinner party's safe bet. It will be a hit, I promise!

DAJON'S DELICIOUS SHRIMP DIJON

1-1/2 lbs large shrimp, cleaned and deveined
1-2 tbsp (or to taste) minced fresh garlic
4 tbsp butter
1/2 tsp (or to taste) dried chili pepper flakes
1-2 tbsp (or to taste) Dijon mustard
1/4 cup fresh lemon juice
1/4 cup fresh parsley, chopped
1/2 tsp salt
1/2 tsp ground black pepper
1/2 cup Italian-style breadcrumbs
grated Parmesan cheese (optional)

In a large sauté pan, cook shrimp, chili flakes, garlic, and butter over medium heat until shrimp are pink and cooked through.
Blend mustard, bread crumbs, lemon juice, parsley, and salt and pepper into shrimp mixture.
Stir and heat thoroughly.
Sprinkle grated parmesan cheese on top and serve immediately.

For dinner, I serve it with a vermicelli or white rice. For an appetizer, I serve it by itself. Either way, it's absolutely delicious!

Chapter 18

Hamster Hell

When I first told my brother Johnny that I was going to write a memoir, he said, "What are you going to do once you have told all of the stories we've heard *a hundred times*" (he exaggerated quite a lot, I guess it's just a family trait that we're stuck with!). I told him that unfortunately, a week doesn't go by that fails to give me another chapter to write. And honestly, I just thought that since I'm giving you all my favorite recipes, many of which I'm stealing (with approval of course, and which I've eaten and enjoyed too many times to count) from friends and family, there really is no end to my memoirs.

Which means that these stories can just go on and on. Case in point: last Saturday morning.

Our daughter Mollie ran into the house after going to a birthday party/sleepover at the home of one of her fellow Girl Scouts, Marissa. It was only about 8:30 a.m., and Sven and I were still (shockingly!) in bed, just about ready to get up. She was so excited! Marissa's dad is a professional pet breeder and trainer. They have about every single animal that will fit in a suburban ranch home. Their house always has a plethora of hedgehogs, snakes, chameleons, pot-bellied pigs, flying Australian rat-looking things, and the list goes on. Who needs to go to the zoo when you have a friend like Marissa?

From time to time, when I walk into Marissa's house to pick up Mollie, I feel kind of sorry for Marissa's mom. Her dad seems to be a great guy, and they seem to have a great relationship. But I always think back to the day they got married and wonder if the vows she took not only included "for better or worse, for richer or poorer, in sickness and in health," but also "for hedgehogs and snakes or chameleons and pigs"? But hey, it's none of my business, and whatever works between couples is just fine with me. Furthermore, who the heck am I to criticize any relationship?! Any fool who could marry P.D. twice should just keep her old mouth shut when it comes to relationship counseling.

Well, Mollie had already begun to almost hyperventilate as she told us that her life would not be worth living until she had a Russian dwarf hamster as a pet just like Marissa had. I thought it was a joke. Did you even know that there were midget hamsters from Russia? Can you imagine all those little rodents having to travel so far just to become someone's pet in America? I immediately began to wonder when a family of Russian dwarf hamsters was going to have their own reality show on TLC?

To her defense, she had actually been really good tolerating all the hormonal hell her older sister had been putting the entire family through these last few months. In fact, Sven had spent the afternoon just the day before putting Maggie's door back on the hinges after it had finally fallen off after being slammed for the thousandth time.

Mollie had also just gotten all A's on her report card, and we won't even talk about Maggie's. (She is always a "work in progress.") So, Sven just looked at me and then I sadly looked back at him and gave him the nod, indicating that we both knew what the heck was going to come out of my mouth next. In hindsight, I wish to God that we could have taken the moment back and just pretended to still be sleeping. Then, who knows if this whole thing might have just lost steam, and she would have lost interest in teeny bitty rats from a foreign country and found another thing to bug her mother and father about.

But noooo, we both caved in and I put on a pair of my favorite, very worn, "holey" skinny jeans (with an elastic waistband, of course). We drove over to the local Pet Utopia to spend about $150 on all the crap we needed for our "free" midget Russian hamster, and then we went over to Marissa's to pick up this fabulously intelligent, fun, easily trainable, sweet rodent. I couldn't hold onto my enthusiasm as we walked into the very pretty, perfectly decorated house, ducking to not get hit in the head by flying Australian bat-like creatures.

When we got "Ernie" home, Mollie hurriedly set up the cage, bedding, and walk-in closet for all the Russian midget rat clothing (complete with fur hats, long coats, and snow boots). She was so excited that: #1 – she had something that her older sister didn't have, #2 – she got yet another thing she wanted with minimal begging or chores around the house, and #3 – Ernie was pretty darn cute if you can forget the fact that his eyes were beady and that even though you could give him any fancy-schmancy name in the book, he is and always will be a R-A-T!

Our two overweight Chihuahuas were not overly thrilled with the newest member of the Ray household. Even though they had never seen anything like Ernie, I think they were just concerned over the fact that he may take away their daily portions of brisket and turkey.

Well, our "pet adoption bliss" is currently in the Guinness Book of Records as the fastest dying moment of "pet bliss" (we call it P.B.) in the world. As soon as Mollie opened the box and her immigrant rat ran into his newly designed home, Mollie decided to hold him for the first time to pet him, probably while lovingly telling him all the hopes and dreams she had for him.

Ernie had the nerve to not want to leave his newly decorated home. Mollie tried for an entire four minutes before she called for me to help get the hamster out of the cage. I told her that I was indeed a hamster expert, because about thirty years ago, Johnny and I had four hamsters (Romeo and Juliet and Adam and Eve), which made me a virtual hamster trainer and rodent therapist.

So, here I am, showing my 11-year old the proven "get your hamster out of the cage" technique. Ernie decided to grab onto my finger with the sharpest teeth I've ever seen. I screamed so loud, people taking a shower in Peoria could have heard me. I then started running around the house screaming and crying, flinging my hand around trying to get this disgusting Russian rat to detach from my hand. Ernie, who was quickly renamed "El Diablo, the Rat from Hell," wouldn't let go for anything. I was psychotically running from room to room screaming, while Mollie and Maggie were psychotically running behind me screaming with me in stereo, trying to save their Mom, the "rat expert!"

Finally (it seemed like about an hour and a half – but, really was about 2-1/2 minutes), Sven left his computer screen and said in his usual deadpan manner, "Here Hon, let me get that rat off you.'" I looked at him, with tears streaming down my face, totally disgusted with what could have been a reel from a disgusting 70s rat movie, with El Diablo still attached to my bleeding finger. Sven calmly pried him off of me, opened the cage drawer, and stuck him back into his cage.

Once Sven shut the door on the damn designer cage, it was never reopened again by any inhabitant of the Ray household. We couldn't even talk about it. I believe that, innately, we knew that discussing it would just bring back the horror of that Saturday morning. It was definitely better left unsaid. The girls and I avoided any contact beyond feeding and funneling in water through the bars of the cage. Sven started making references to El Diablo as a "prisoner of conscience" and his cage as a "pet gulag of solitary confinement." This is when I knew that he was starting to lose it, but also getting a few chuckles out of the absurdity.

So, what the heck did we do to this Russian dwarf hamster that was literally in solitary confinement? Not being the sort of people who the members of PETA would be offended by, simultaneously as we were sliding water and food into his cage (very carefully, with 5-inch-thick gloves on), we were all trying to figure out who the heck would want this disgusting creature. Marissa's family, of course had a "no rat back" policy; and my idea of just letting him go off into the "suburban wild" wasn't going to fly because it was the middle of a miserable winter.

One day soon after our acquisition, when the kids were at Sunday School, Sven and I even sneaked back to Pet Utopia and tried to give the store back the cage, the food and the clothing. Since it had only been a few days, I even had all my receipts and didn't want a dime back. They could have kept it all if they would just take the rat away, "no questions asked."

The manager couldn't have been older than 19 and was dressed as if Morticia from the Addams Family was her fashion icon (I had to remind myself that it was February). She spoke in such a monotone voice that I'm sure the Prozac level in her bloodstream was right beneath "stage catatonic." Sven, thinking that this was a hilarious situation to be in, took the cage, which was covered in an old beach towel, and said something like, "I'd like to introduce to you 'El Diablo,' or you could call him 'Damien.'" When you think of it, not a very good thing to say when you're trying to pawn off a rat with sword-sized teeth.

Everyone in the store just laughed when they saw this rat gnawing on the wire cage. It was more creepy than funny. But Morticia looked at us and, in as much of a monotone as you can get, said, "Sorry, we don't take anyone else's rodents." She continued to drone, "We have the strictest standards in rodents and this would be totally against Pet Utopia policies." Sven and I put the towel around the cage, took all our miscellaneous gerbil paraphernalia, and slid out of Utopia as quickly as we could.

All of a sudden, by the grace of God, Maggie had an idea. One of her middle school science teachers had a huge cage in her class with about ten rodents, lizards, and such. Her sweet teacher was amenable to giving Ernie a home, where he is, in fact, residing today.

Months later, our nightmares have been reduced to a minimum, and I can tell you that the only good that came from this mishap is that neither of our daughters have ever mentioned the idea of having another pet in our home.

Just as a side note, I thought it was hilarious that when I had Sven read the chapter for his now "have to read before it's published" policy, he said, in his droll way, "Hon, you need to home in more on the absurdity of the moment. You really didn't do it justice!" What does that tell you?!?

My wonderful friend Kathy made these the other night for Bunko. Everyone went absolutely insane over these and I just thought the recipe would be perfect for this chapter. Instead of "comfort food," how about "comfort booze"? It doesn't get much more "comfortable" than these delicious pudding shots with vanilla vodka and Bailey's. Enjoy — and please don't drive after 2 of these.

KATHY'S FAMOUS JELL-O PUDDING SHOTS

(2) 3.5-oz packages chocolate instant pudding
1-1/2 cups whole milk
1/2 cup Bailey's Irish Cream
1/2 cup Kahlua
1/2 cup vanilla vodka
16-oz tub Cool Whip

Combine pudding and liquid ingredients together and mix well. Fold in the Cool Whip and spoon the mix into plastic or glass shot cups and freeze.

Chapter 19

The Very Deep Love Of A Daddy Gone Amok

It's amazing how many things a woman is able to repress. It's also amazing to me how, when, and where the repressed memories can rear their ugly (and with me, just plain bizarre) heads.

Today, as I was drinking coffee with Sven at say, 7:46 a.m. this morning while watching a segment of our favorite news show, "Morning Joe," Joe and Mika were talking about a comet that was to appear this evening at 11:50 p.m. (Eastern Standard Time – not suburban Central time).

All of a sudden, Sven said, "Wow, Honey! That sounds great! We should...." And then he stopped himself, turned bright red, and said in a sheepish tone while looking at the ground, "Oh, never mind...." At that instant, I'm sure that repressed memory #1,876 came back to both of us from the repressed memory cemetery (R.M.C.) at the same time. And we just looked at each other and, in stereo, we both cracked up, laughing so hard that tears were streaming down both our faces.

So, let's go back down memory lane about nine years, when Sven and I first got married. Things were going swimmingly even though P.D. tried to rear his ugly head every time the moon was full (coincidence?) and even with the day-to-day dealings (also known as Suburban Psycho Dramas), sibling rivalry extraordinaire, raging hormones, or simply "tweens" dealing with a new Dad.

It never ceases to amaze me how two children who come from the same two parents and are in the same exact environment, can end up so totally different. I always call it the "Quintessential Genetic Crapshoot". I'm sure that it's the same in your household. Mollie has always had this pain-in-the-butt way about her, thinking about What's Next? It's gotten so bad that I've renamed our beautiful youngest daughter to incorporate this talent into her name. Because the kid always seems to have an agenda, the mathematical equation I made up went like this:

Mollie + Agenda = Magenda

On the other hand, Maggie is a kid who, once she homes in on something that she loves, it ends up being a bit obsessive. Whether or not it's Broadway musicals, television shows, a sugary cereal with chocolate in the middle, whatever.

Well, this particular month nine years ago, the obsession happened to be astronomy. She was taking a course in middle school that she adored. She then decided to save all of her babysitting money to buy a cheap telescope, wore a goofy Indiana Jones hat (I'm not sure what that was all about, but we went with it), and started watching the Discovery channel even more than SpongeBob Square Pants (there is a God!).

One day that week, Sven came home from work and very excitedly told us all at dinner that the latest comet named after some Greek god was going to create a meteor shower. He then explained his plan to clean up our 15-year-old, $2,000 convertible ("Old Blue") and have it ready for us to drive to the exact location where, according to all the scientists, the best view of the meteor shower was going to be.

I thought Maggie was going to have kittens. She just screamed with delight, and said "Oh, Daddy, that sounds fantastic! I can't wait! I'll get my telescope, my camera, blankets, and everything else ready!" Mollie and I just looked very calmly at both Sven and Maggie, and I said (in the best monotone voice I could muster), "Oh, you two should have a wonderful time! It sounds very exciting!"

Sven stopped, put his fork down right by his grilled chicken chopped salad, and asked, "What are you talking about, Honey? You and Mollie are coming, too!" Then he continued, "This only happens one time every 18,427 years, you can't miss this. You'd regret your decision for the rest of your life!" Looking at my excited, dear husband and our older, salivating child, I conceded, realizing that I couldn't let them have this experience alone. Of course they needed us to go with them.

Finally, the date arrived and Sven and Maggie had found the exact location where the view would be the pinnacle of cosmos fireworks. The father-daughter team plotted the cosmic exploration so carefully, Carl Sagan would have been proud. We packed the small four-seater so much that it looked like we were on our way to Canada instead of 124 miles away to a small Missouri town.

Sven and I each took a half-day off from our jobs. We ate dinner at 3:00 p.m. and then went straight to bed, setting our alarm clocks for 1:30 a.m. Mollie and I moaned and groaned as we tried to fit in the back seat of the little, overstuffed convertible while the space explorers, wearing matching "Indiana Jones" hats (Sven had to buy one to match Maggie's), gingerly hopped into the front seat of the $2,000 convertible with the top down.

For the next 2 hours, Mollie and I froze our butts off, getting beaten up by the wind. But we both decided to stop whining and moaning, because it was useless (they couldn't hear us anyway). So, feeling totally defeated, we slid down into our seats with the covers over our head, while the two astronomers were plotting the precise spot at which to see the heavenly fireworks. It seemed like we were on the road for about 3-1/2 days, but thankfully, at 3:46 a.m., we arrived at an empty field in the middle of frigging nowhere.

We thought for sure that herds of space explorers were going to beat us to this "perfect spot." Heck, I thought news reporters from all over the world, and probably the entire staff of the Discovery Channel, were going to be there, too. To our surprise, it was eerily quiet. We couldn't believe we were the only ones there. How could everyone in the space community miss this huge event?!

More than anything, I wish I would have remembered to bring one of my many disposable cameras (basically, because I've never really been tech savvy enough to learn how to use those "simple," every-parent-in-the-world-can-use-one-cameras, except for Sven and me!), because honestly, to say that it wasn't a pretty sight is the understatement of the millennium. After being scrunched up in a convertible in the middle of the night for over two hours, it took Mollie and me several minutes to literally fall out of the car and "un-pretzel" our bodies. Indiana Jones and his sidekick looked a little wind-beaten and tired themselves, but were still pretty excited that "Old Blue" had "landed."

They both systematically set up the blankets, telescopes, and video cameras to capture the cataclysmic event, and then we waited. Then we waited some more, and then even more. When the sun started to come out, Indiana and Indiana Junior looked at each other, and defeatedly said, "OK, we'd better go. It didn't happen…."

Mollie and I didn't say a word. I think that not only were we frozen and numb, and so tired we couldn't make a fist even if we tried, but deep down, we felt a little sorry for them. We just silently climbed back into the back seat, hunkered down on the floor of Old Blue, and covered our heads for the ride back to civilization and our beds.

It was a very quiet ride back home. What I couldn't get out of my mind, but wouldn't have dared say, was that when we finally got home and I looked into the sky, you know what? I bet if anything glorious had happened, we would have been able to see the same thing had we just sat in our comfortable lawn chairs outside.

I kind of made up this little salad by just adding all my favorite things into a bowl and mixing it up…isn't that what we always do?! But whenever I make it, Sven goes absolutely crazy — in a good way, so I thought it would be nice to give the recipe to my BFFs. Feel free to change it up anyway you'd like. Just let me know what you did so I can tweak this recipe, as well.

THE BEST DADDY IN THE WORLD'S FAVORITE CHICKEN CHOPPED SALAD

¾ cups Muenster or cheddar cheese (sharp or mild)
2 grilled chicken breasts, thinly sliced
salt and pepper
¼ cup poppyseed salad dressing
¼ cup ranch salad dressing
¾ cup celery
¾ cup onion
¾ cup cauliflower
¾ cup broccoli
¾ cup carrots

Chop and mix together in a large bowl the celery, onion, cauliflower, broccoli, and carrots.

(Just as an FYI, I've been going to Trader Joe's or the grocery store and purchasing the veggies already chopped up. They are fairly inexpensive, and the time you save is well worth it — along with not getting carpal tunnel syndrome from all the chopping.)

Add ¾ cups of cubed Muenster or sharp or mild cheddar cheese (whichever you prefer). Then add 2 thinly sliced, grilled chicken breasts, and salt and pepper to taste. (I get these at Trader Joe's as well, when i'm in a hurry.)

Mix together ¼ cup of your favorite poppyseed salad dressing (mine is Marzetti's) and ¼ cup of your favorite ranch dressing (mine is Kraft peppercorn ranch) and toss into the salad.

Serve immediately and enjoy.

Another FYI: because of all of the "crunchiness, this salad has staying power and can be served the following day and still be delicious!

Chapter 20

Everyone Has Their Own Expertise

By now you must know how much I love my husband. This may sound a little sad, but I honestly think he is the first man to really love me. I mean really truly love and like the person that I am, with all of my thousands of flaws and neuroses. Even the jerk that I married and divorced twice and had two beautiful daughters with — I would bet a million dollars that he never really loved me. I don't know if it was anything that I did wrong (except for the fact that I had the worst taste and judgment of anyone on the planet). There are people on this planet that are just incapable of true love. That's as sad as it gets, don't you think?

Now, looking back twelve years, I think that he just saw me as a kind of a meal ticket (a very, very small meal). Let's just call me a "Happy Meal ticket" kind of gal. I don't know what the deal was, but it has to be something like that.

I promised myself that I wouldn't talk about P.D. at all in my second book, or if I had to, I'd keep it to a minimum. But things keep popping up that I would be remiss not tell all of my new BFFs. I know that if anyone would appreciate how ludicrous life can be, it would be you!

So, last week after the New Year holiday, Sven was sweet enough to purchase us two tickets to a concert that I really wanted to go to. It was a beautiful night, and just what the doctor ordered after an unbelievably hectic holiday. We doubled with a very sweet couple, went to a "hole-in-the-wall" Thai restaurant, and were enjoying the concert immensely when I decided *of course* that I had to use the restroom. I actually strategized about it for about 8 minutes before I felt safe enough to attempt to find the restroom.

Digressing yet again: do you know how sometimes at a show you know you really have to pee, but God forbid that, for any reason, you might miss any of your favorite songs? You also want to make triple-sure that you're taking the *right* route to make certain that you can get back to your seat afterward without making the other concertgoers stand up and grunt at you for making them stand up. It's all a very serious business.

Anyway, I was in the restroom, standing in line with other brave women (or women who just had one too many beers during the concert), when all of a sudden I saw one of Sven's oldest and dearest friends, Beth. I gave her a hug and wished her a Happy New Year, and we talked for a minute about how great the concert was.

Beth looked at me, and she said, "Oh, Laura, I have to tell you about the strangest thing that happened on Christmas Eve. I was going to call you, but things have been so insane, it slipped my mind." I didn't know what the heck it could be, and I'm never shocked anymore by any news I hear (*Just wait — this time even I was!*), she continued, "Don and I were with a group of friends on Christmas Eve at this cute neighborhood bar in South St. Louis. We were just talking, eating, and drinking when all of a sudden a really strange guy just comes up to us out of nowhere. He rudely interrupts us and starts talking to us."

She then explained, "We were trying to be nice to him — heck, it was Christmas Eve. But he was just so strange. And then all of a sudden, out of nowhere, he blurts out, "Hey, do you know a guy by the name of Sven?" She said, "We just looked at him and said, "Yes, as a matter of fact, he and his wife Laura are very good friends of ours. Why do you ask?" She continued, "All of a sudden, his eyes opened really wide, he pushed out his chest as if he was really proud of himself, and he said, 'Well, let me introduce myself to you. *Hi, I'm Psycho Dick!*'"

She looked at me and shook her head, and said, "We were all kind of speechless, Laura. We really didn't know what to say. And all of a sudden, Don looked at him, and you know how soft-spoken he is; he just said in the kindest way he could, 'Well, I don't think that is something you should be very proud of, and I definitely wouldn't be bragging to anyone about it!'"

Do you even believe it?! He was actually *bragging* about being P.D.? It was like his twisted, sick claim to fame. Oh, my God, how pathetic is that? Like I said before, nothing ever really shocks me anymore, but this sure did.

OK, I'm finished digressing, so now it's time for me to start the actual story. As I said before, Sven loves me, even knowing all about my warts (figuratively and literally), neuroses, cellulite ass, etc., and for that I will always be eternally grateful to him. I guess a lot of you can always say that about your spouses, too; but for me it was always a little "foreign," given that I somehow fell for an alien who is proud to call himself Psycho Dick.

About 2 weeks ago, Mollie's soccer league scheduled a game at 9:30 p.m. on a school night. It was insanity. It was cold outside; the girls have to catch the bus every morning at 6:37 a.m., in the dark; homework assignments were reproducing asexually in their backpacks; and, to add insult to injury, the game took place about 35 minutes away from our house.

When I told Sven about the game, he looked at me as if I had just asked him to run the Boston Marathon. He said, "You don't expect me to go to the game, do you?!" I looked at him and said, in my best passive-aggressive tone of voice, "Oh no, Honey, that's fine. Don't worry about me. I'll just go alone and try to find this stupid soccer field and I'll sit in the cold by myself." He looked at me in his defeated "beat me/whip me" style and softly said, "When are we leaving?'"

So, here are Sven and I, sitting in the freezing cold in our cheap Walgreens portable chairs, covered in blankets; sipping from our cold thermos of coffee; watching these tired, little, skinny pre-teens playing soccer at this awful time of night. They were so cute, giving their "all" even though they were freezing and miserable. You just had to love them even more for their sincerity. There was no way in hell that these kids, not being masochists, could actually be enjoying themselves.

We knew that we're not ever going to produce the next Mia Hamm at these stupid games, and that these kids are really never going to end up in the Olympics or win any kind of scholarship (who knows, I could be wrong). I have never been one of those parents who push their daughters into sports.

Please don't get me wrong. If the kids want to do anything at all – soccer, field hockey, swimming, underwater basket weaving — you can count me in to drive; cook a Heath Bar cake for the Better-Luck-Next-Time party; not miss any game; pay *stupid* amounts of money for head gear and uniforms, and then for the necessary physical therapy afterward. But screaming and yelling at the kids for missing a goal is definitely not my thing. Sometimes, the lunacy of some of these Soccer Moms and Dads can be overwhelming.

I know I've told you this before, but just in case you forgot, Sven knows 99.99 percent of everything there is to know about music. He's the kind of guy who hates when people think "St. Louis Blues" refers only to a game played on ice with sticks, and not the great blues music that came from this city and surrounding areas.

But even if you're not into sports, it's impossible to watch these kids play and give it their all and not get totally involved. So, here we are, about 42 minutes into the game, and we have lost all feeling in our limbs. But we're getting into the game. We are both pretty much looking like idiots; every time we open our mouths, we create cold air smoke signals.

The other girls' fathers were actually on the field, acting as coaches and referees and behaving as if this were the final game of the World Cup. But not us — we just looked like Mr. and Mrs. Nanook, trying to stay alive in the midst of a blizzard.

That is when it happened. The score was tied 2 - 2 with only a few minutes left. The girls were in the midst of a long scrimmage, and all of a sudden Sven screamed," *"OK, girls: Stick and move! Stick and move!"*

It could have been in slow motion! Everything just came to a halt. There was total silence. All the tired, worn-out, 87-lb. frozen girls just stopped and stared at Sven and me. The very serious fathers and coaches stopped. And then, all of a sudden, one of the girls on the team asked, in the sweetest voice, "Mollie, *what* does your Daddy want us to do?"

Mollie was huffing and puffing, and said, "I don't know!" And then she looked at him across the field and yelled politely across the field, "Daddy, what are you talking about?"

Sven just looked at me and sheepishly said, "Oh, I don't know. That's just the only sports term that I know, so, I just thought I'd scream it." All eyes were on us when one of the dads looked at him and said, "That's a boxing term, isn't it?" All of a sudden I started giggling so hard that my $12 chair collapsed and I fell to the ground.

The whole slo-mo event was so damn cute, it just tickled the heck out of me. And it goes to show that no one can be an expert on everything. Even though Sven is no sports expert, he loves his daughters (and his wife) very much. Doesn't get much better than that.

For this story, I thought I'd do a great recipe that is *STICKY* and doesn't *MOVE*:

SHARON'S STICKY & DELICIOUS MONKEY BREAD

3 (10 ounce) Pillsbury refrigerated buttermilk biscuits
1/2 cup sugar
1 tablespoon cinnamon
1 cup butter (2 sticks)
1 cup brown sugar
2 teaspoons water
¾ cup pecans

Preheat oven to 350° Place pecans onto the bottom of a buttered bundt pan.
Then quarter one biscuit at a time and roll in cinnamon/sugar mixture.
One by one, place in pan until the bundt pan is filled.
Melt butter and brown sugar, and stir together to mix as well as possible.
Pour evenly over the biscuits.
Place the bundt pan on top of a cookie sheet to avoid a mess in your oven!

Bake for 45 to 50 minutes until golden brown.

Hint: You may need to put aluminum foil on the top at the end of the baking, due to the top of the bread getting too brown while the middle is still gooey.

Enjoy! This is a killer, sticky recipe.

Chapter 21

OK, American Medical Association Add a New Disease, Please!

One of the chapters that readers of my first book tell me they relate to most is the one where I talk about my made-up disease, "Generosity Tourette's," or G.T. If you haven't read my first book , I'll quickly explain it to you. It's a disease that makes well-meaning but poorly considered thoughts turn into actual words that spew from your mouth uncontrollably.

For example, "Oh, you need a place to live? I'm sure you could live in our basement for a while." Or, "Oh, you're broke? Well, I get paid on Friday; how about if I split my paycheck with you to help out until you get back on your feet?" Sometimes it's even less conspicuous spewing, such as, "Don't worry, I'll drive you to radiation for the next three weeks and make sure that your family has dinner on the table every day until May." Or what is even worse, when you end up spewing things like, "I'm sure that my sweet husband wouldn't mind deejaying for your daughter's wedding;" or, "My brother would certainly take your small criminal case for free!"

Horrible, self-serving, get-yourself-in-trouble-the-minute-the-words-come-out-of-your-mouth words.

So many women have said to me, yes, they too are victims of this terrible affliction. I even give out big, hot pink lapel buttons (especially when I'm doing book signings and visiting book clubs) that simply say, "GOT G.T.?" (Total strangers come up to me and tell me they know exactly what I'm talking about.)

So, having already made up one disease, I think I'm on a roll. Let me also preface this by saying that I certainly don't want to offend anyone, and, having mental illness in my family, I'm definitely aware of the destruction it wreaks on a family and certainly on the one who suffers from it. That said, I'm almost certain that, as with G.T., I am not the only one who is afflicted with the new made-up disease that I call "Guilt Schizophrenia." We can call this one "G.S." for short.

Let me give you a quick run-down on the symptoms. This one is a bit trickier than G.T. because it has a little "Mommy OCD and ADD" sprinkled in it. It's basically those little tiny voices in a mom's head, talking to each other and convincing you to change your plans anywhere from 3 to 176 times a day. These voices will say things like, If you don't cancel your luncheon with your friends so that you can pick up your daughter and her three friends at their hangout (which happens to be only a quarter-mile from your home), something terribly bad will happen. Or your kid will end up spending so much time walking (God forbid!) that she won't have time to finish her homework or study for her algebra quiz.

Or perhaps you are driving toward a nice neighborhood restaurant to meet your husband, who happens to be named Sven, and then suddenly *that voice* tells you that you really should just make an appearance at the Made by Me Jewelry/Pampered Chef combo party that several of your "mom" friends invited you to, with all the money going to the PTA, and it won't take long, so you could probably do both. And then *that* voice reminds you that you haven't made a meal for your sick neighbor for over a week and you haven't even made a homemade meal for the kids in forever, but then *that* voice tells you that you could probably order three really nice meals at the restaurant that you're meeting your husband at after you attend the jewelry/cooking combo party. It goes on and on. Those teeny tiny voices just never shut up!

Those little voices can end up driving not only you but everyone around you completely nuts. It's gotten to the point where my poor husband will just pull over to the side of the road in the middle of his nightly 12-mile journey from his store to our house and call me in a controlled, frustrated scream, "Where the hell do you want me to be? I'm not moving this car another inch until you tell me where you want me!" And "What the heck do you want me to bring home?" And sometimes, "We're doing what? Have you totally lost your mind?!"

I know that everyone reading this right now has a bit of this affliction. I really haven't made up anything — I've just put a name to it. Maybe, just maybe, by quickly putting it "out there," we'll all be able to nip it in the bud, discover a drug to fix it, or mix some kind of killer low-calorie martini that will put those little voices to rest. Pharmaceutical companies from all over the continent take note: here's another potential revenue stream.

If you don't completely understand my new made-up disease, let me offer several more scenarios where the voices take over. See if you can relate at all. And if you can't, I promise I won't bring it up again, because it's all pretty embarrassing.

You find yourself in a state of shock, screaming after a really long day at work, "You kicked your sister in the knee and pulled her hair out of her head and look — Oh, my God, I can see an actual bald spot!" Then you continue, "OK, You are so grounded! Go to your room and stay there for six hours." (Two seconds later, the little voices tell you that you're going to have to totally back down on her punishment because, as the voices remind you)…"Oh, you're supposed to be at your Girl Scout meeting in ten minutes and we promised to bring the treats this week." So you continue, "Fine, then, just promise you'll never do it again and tell your sister you are very sorry and we will just find her a hat to cover the bald spot."

Or maybe…

"I know I said that we'd have "family time" tonight and have dinner at the dining room table, but Cathy just called me and needs me to meet her for a cup of coffee. She just found out her husband has been cheating on her. She's hysterical and needs someone to talk to!" (Two seconds later, the little voices were telling me that I'm being a horrible wife and mother, and starving my children.)

"All right, I know you all are craving my chicken parmesan. Fine, I'll call Cathy and tell her I'll meet her for drinks after we eat the chicken parmesan, and then we'll go through your pre-algebra problems, OK?" and "Honey, I'll make you your favorite dessert and we'll eat it together while we watch "Bourne Identity" together for the thousandth time."

Or maybe…

"OK, I want you to know that Daddy and I are going out tonight for 'date night' (for the first time in months because those *little voices* tell you…). "Why don't each of you invite a friend over for pizza. I've left $30 for the delivery person, cake mixes, and frosting so you can all make cupcakes together, rented two movies for you to watch, and bought some craft stuff so you can all make some cool things for Valentine's Day while you're watching movies, eating pizza, and baking your cupcakes." (Those voices tell you that you need to make sure that the kids are having a nice night together with their friends because it's a 3-day holiday and we couldn't afford to go anywhere nice).

A side note to this particular example: the entire evening ended up costing way too much, and 24 minutes into our date, I got a call from Mollie telling me that she was developing welts on her knee and she was worried that she may be coming down with typhoid fever. Those *little voices* in my head made Sven ask the waiter to wrap up our food that hadn't even arrived to our table yet and make it "to go." We drove back home to find both of our daughters perfectly fine. The welts were just a little poison ivy, and the kids were all thoroughly enjoying their fine and very impromptu slumber party. Who wouldn't?

I could go on, but why bother? The gist of the disease is that we all hear these pain-in-the-butt *little voices* in our heads that continually try to make sure that everyone is happy and safe. When our plans don't work, we try to change them over and over, ad nauseam, in order to please everyone. The sad thing is that by the time you finally do it and appease the damn *little voices* (which I have heard are multi-lingual), you have succeeded in driving yourself and everyone around you crazy. And, the saddest thing of all, is that you end up… not enjoying anything!

It reminds me of a plaque given to me years ago by a creepy old optometrist who was a customer of mine in South Bumble.F&%@ and who continually tried to get me into bed with him (eeeeeeek!). It said,

"Those Who Try to Please Everyone Will Be An Ultimate Failure" (Isn't it odd that a 82-year-old dirty old man who I shared a cup of coffee with once a week knew me well enough back then to buy me a wall hanging with that particular saying?) I guess these voices have been with me for decades!

This affliction is, I'm sure, predominantly female oriented. Aren't all of my made-up diseases?!

I'll let you know about all the medical statistics and cures just as soon as the AMA gives me a call. Maybe the next time we meet, if you have any clue as to how to make these *little voices* go away, by all means – I beg of you, for my sanity and the sanity of those around me — please let me know. If you've never met me before and you don't know what I look like, I'll be the one in the fetal position under the table somewhere, waiting for the phone to ring to let me know what I'm supposed to do or where I'm supposed to be next.

These are so darn delicious that you will definitely feel guilty. But we're all going to feel guilty no matter what we do, so why not do so with these killer cookies!?

TAYLOR'S GUILT-RIDDEN NUTTY CARAMEL BALLS

Cookie:
2-1/2 cups flour
1 cup sugar
2 sticks salted butter, melted
¼ cup chopped pecans

Coating:
2 bags caramels, unwrapped
3 tablespoons water
2 cups chopped pecans

Preheat oven to 350 degrees.

Mix flour, sugar, melted butter, and chopped pecans in large mixing bowl. Roll mixture into approximately 1-1/2 to 2-inch balls and place them on an ungreased cookie sheet.

Bake for 10 to 12 minutes or until golden brown. (I usually turn them 6 minutes into the baking process to make sure that the bottoms don't get too brown.)

Take the cookies out and let them cool for at least 30 minutes. When cookies are cooled, place the caramels and water in a large, microwave-safe bowl and melt the caramels at 1 minute at a time, stirring thoroughly after every few additions, until caramels are completely melted.

On a large sheet of waxed paper, place the bowl of melted caramels and a bowl of the chopped pecans right next to the cookies.
Gently drop each cookie into caramel and then roll it in the chopped pecans. Set on the waxed paper until the caramel cools.
Enjoy!

CHAPTER 22

Hear Ye Hear Ye
I Am Hereby Changing My
"There Are Two Types Of People
In The World" Theory
(Did you notice the rhyme?)

So, for years and years I always said that there were two types of people in this world. So are you thinking, Democrat or Republican, or maybe, Christian or Non-Christian, or maybe even left-or right-handed? Nope, that's not it. Ok, so the two types of people in the world according to Laura Ray are those who love White Castle Cheeseburgers and those who absolutely hate them. There is never a happy median where people are indifferent to those little belly bombers. You either love them or hate them!

I, Laura Ray, must admit that I am on the "love them" side and so are Mollie and Maggie. But to be completely honest, I haven't been able to eat them for a very long time.

Right after I took the girls and finally left P.D., I started a little twisted family tradition. We went to about ten sessions of the United Way therapy group called "Kids in the Middle." I was trying to be as pro-active as possible, and didn't want to turn on the television set fourteen years later to see my beautiful daughters on the Montel Williams show showing America their body carvings and multiple piercings.

After the very sad sessions, which I think actually ended up teaching the girls a deep-seated empathy towards kids from divorced families and somehow giving them the knowledge of how good they have it after all; we would go straight to a neighborhood White Castle and eat our numerous burgers and cheese fries while we talked about the happenings that evening. God forbid I took the kids to Whole Foods (aka: "Whole Paycheck") and we'd all split a tofu burger with sprouts and avocado…no, not me; I decided to comfort my kids with greasy food with many condiments to choose from.

I'm not sure if it is just repressed sad memories or that my stomach is just getting pickier as it's getting older; but I haven't been able to stomach the food from that white little building ever since.

I was very comfortable dividing the entire world in those two categories until last night, when I decided that it's about time for my theory to change.

Last night, Sven and I were invited to a birthday dinner party for one of Sven's closest friends. He is a part of a group of talented musicians that love to "jam" every week, write music together, and then play on each other's independently made CDs.

It's a great group of friends even though Sven and I are the oldest ones in the group. It's a little humbling knowing that you are hanging out with people who hadn't even been born when you graduated from high school. But, these twenty people happen to be the most giving, wonderful friends and we all just "clicked" the minute Sven introduced me to everyone.

After reading all of my chapters and knowing about all of the stupid and embarrassing things I've done in my life, this definitely pales in comparison; and most of the time, it really doesn't seem to matter at all. But last night, I realized that there are some things that I can't overlook. Even when I try to act as cool as I can, sometimes I just lose it, and it's really not pretty when it happens and my inner "dork-dom" just takes over.

To be fair to myself (which we rarely are, don't you agree?), I may have been at a disadvantage, because the party was on a Tuesday evening, which just so happened to be after a very long and depressing day at work, getting the kids to school by 6:30 a.m., having to pick up Mollie during lunch because her body decided to produce strange lumps on her legs and arms (fyi to my best friends: they went away as strangely as they popped up – but thankfully not until the doctor saw them, took pictures of them for the AMA, and then told us that she just has a very strange body that reacts strangely to allergies.) Mollie has always been able to take a few years off my life span with her strange body. So, needless to say, I was exhausted, looked like hell, and was 35 minutes late because I wanted to make dinner for the girls, feed the dogs, and make the Caesar salad that the birthday boy requested.

Compared to the other women at the party, I looked like a tired old hag. There was a beautiful, size 0 yoga instructor, two women who worked for charity organizations, and the hostess who just married her doting, sweet, madly in love husband.

It was a lovely night on the whole, which the doctor definitely had ordered. I had a glass of cranberry juice and vodka over crushed ice (absolutely delicious and I knew that I wouldn't be getting a urinary tract infection anytime soon thanks to the cranberry juice!), was able to calm down, and started to enjoy myself.

After the wonderful dinner (they are all "foodies," too!) The guys all went downstairs in the basement to play their music, while the girls all went to the kitchen to clean up the delicious New Orleans themed dinner.

As I felt myself fading fast, I started gathering my huge salad bowl and utensils to stick in the car, so that I wouldn't forget them and that way, the lovely hostess wouldn't have to wash them.

As I went out the front door, I saw a large photo of John Lennon and Yoko Ono. I don't know why, but I just involuntarily blurted out, "God, I've always loved John Lennon so much, but boy, do I hate Yoko!!!!"

I then continued with, "Hell, I laugh and honk everytime I see that bumper sticker that says, "I STILL BLAME YOKO!"

With that, all of the young and hip women looked at me like I was an alien. In "stereo" they all said, "Gosh Laura, WE LOVE YOKO!!!",

"We think she is so talented, loved John so much, and her singing voice is beautiful!!!!" "How can you possibly say bad things about Yoko????!!!!????"

I felt my face flush, I was completely speechless (which you all know by now does not happen very often) and just looked at these 20 and 30-something gorgeous women and very sheepishly tried to explain myself by saying, "Well….I just always thought that Yoko never had any true girlfriends, and didn't you hear the rumor of how John and Yoko met?" I continued to ramble, "His sweet wife (Cynthia) invited the homeless Yoko into their home to feed her, and then Yoko ended up sleeping with John?" I was now on a roll and my voice started to get involuntarily loud, "and then, how about how she treated Julian? Hell, Yoko cheated him out of all kinds of money and I think I heard that he wasn't even allowed to go to his funeral?!?" My final points were, "And honestly, don't you think that she was the main reason why the Beatles broke up and then once they were married, she set up a mistress to be with John when she no longer wanted to sleep with him….YUCK! And furthermore, don't you think her voice sounds like a cat that had been smooshed under a huge garage door?"

If you could have just seen the looks on these girls faces?!? I think they were in shock at the emotional mess I had just become right before their very eyes. I just didn't know what else to say or do. I ended up not saying a darn thing for the rest of the night…I think I may have been experiencing a little bit of Post Traumatic Beatles Shock (aka: P.T.B.S.). All of a sudden, I felt like I didn't fit into this group of new friends anymore at all. It was a very strange feeling.

An hour later as we were driving home, I think I was still perplexed beyond belief, and when I was telling Sven this horrific story, he looked at me and very calmly said, "Hon, it's just a generational thing…you just can't take it so personally."

So, I thought about his brilliant, yet very short counsel for a few minutes, and then regrouped. "OK then", I said, "I guess I'll just change my entire criteria on how I divide the universe." " Instead of the "Love White Castle/Hate White Castle" psychology study, I'll just change it to the "Those Who Love Yoko Ono" vs. the "Those Who Can't Stand Her."

Next time I meet you at a book fair or women's club, please let me know where you stand on this new study of mine. I promise, I won't hold it against you no matter how you feel.

This is the salad that our good friend Davey and many other people love. I bring it to parties all of the time (whether or not they like Yoko)

DAVEY'S FAVORITE CAESAR SALAD WITH GRILLED SHRIMP

10 jumbo shrimp, deveined in shell, raw
extra-virgin olive oil, about 1/3 cup for brushing
coarse salt and black pepper
1 lemons, halved

Preheat griddle or grill pan over high heat.
Butterfly shrimp by slicing almost through lengthwise, but leave shell on shrimp. This will keep the shrimp tender while grilling over such high heat.
Brush shrimps with oil, season with salt and pepper and grill 2 minutes on each side, until shells are hot pink and shrimp is opaque.
Place lemons on grill the last minute. The heat will release the juice from the lemons. To serve, squeeze grilled lemon wedges over shrimp.
Set aside to place on top of salad.

Salad:
1 large head of Romaine lettuce
1 cup of grated Parmesan cheese
1 cup of shredded provel cheese
1½ cups of your favorite garlic & cheese croutons
1 tbsp. of black pepper

Salad Dressing: (You can either make this killer dressing, or if you don't have time, just buy your favorite Caesar Salad dressing in the produce department at your grocery store)
In blender, mix together the following:
2 anchovy fillets
2 fresh garlic cloves
1 cup mayonnaise
1/4 cup half-and-half cream or 1/4 cup milk
1/3 cup grated parmesan cheese
2 tablespoons fresh squeezed lemon juice
1 tablespoon Dijon mustard (Hellman's Dijonnaise is best!)
½ teaspoon of salt
½ teaspoon of pepper

2 teaspoons Worcestershire sauce
¼ cup of buttermilk or half-and-half, for thinning if needed
refrigerate until you serve the salad. toss the salad with the croutons, Parmesan
cheese, provel cheese and salad dressing.
Place the grilled shrimp on top of the salad and serve.

Hope you love it as much as Davey!

Chapter 23

Stockholm, Get Ready for Laura Ray

I have to be honest and admit to you, my new best friends, that I am no rocket scientist. I've always been one of those hard-working "worker bees" who only got Bs all through school, and it still was never easy. I can't even say that I had book sense but no street smarts — just look at my past: marrying an abusive alcoholic not once, but twice — a man who already had five children from his first marriage. I could go on and on about all the things I have done that will prove to you that I'm not the brightest bulb out there! But, during the road trip that I took with Sven this weekend (to a lovely wedding in Columbus, Ohio), I talked non-stop (just ask him) about two brilliant ideas I have on how to make our world a better place.

As I said before, with working about 60 hours a week, raising teens, and having a very busy hubby, I rarely find time to pee. So, after reading this brilliant, *and yes, more serious than my usual* chapter, if any of you would like to take any of my ideas and run with them to make our world a better place, I will be honored. In fact, I will be so damn proud of you that I promise I'll buy a ticket, *coach, of course*, to be in one of the first 100 rows in Stockholm to watch when you win the coveted Nobel Peace Prize.

The first idea that I bored Sven with (during the time when we were accidentally about 42 miles in the wrong direction, in Nowhereville, Illinois) is what I'm going to call, *Beautify Jamaica Mon Day*. Let me go back just a little and tell you that Sven goes to Jamaica at least twice a year on business. He and his partner have produced some CDs with several fabulous musicians down there, and *whether he wants to or not*, he goes down there to give royalty checks to these musicians. (What a fun job that would be! I would feel like the third step-cousin of the guy who knocks on the door from the Publisher's Clearing House if I were the one handing over a bit of money that means a whole lot to a middle-class Jamaican!)

Last summer, Sven decided to take me on his fun trip. He refuses to stay at the all-inclusive resorts, because he loves the country so much and hates the fact that locals don't own the resorts. I don't have the hard-core facts, but according to Sven (and since he's been doing business there for over 20 years, I'll quote him), most of those all-inclusives are owned by businesses in other countries, which means that most of the money made from the resorts does not stay in the country. Because of this, we always stay at some quaint, locally owned, very romantic resort instead, which to me is a total win-win! Our favorite, which you all need to try out one day, is called, "Catch a Falling Star." It is beautiful, and the breakfast that they bring to you every morning on the terrace of your private grass hut overlooking these gorgeous cliffs (*can you say "heaven" for $150/night?*) is probably one of the most delicious breakfasts I've ever had!

One afternoon, we decided to drive our rental car to the beach that was known to be Bob Marley's favorite. Sven loves to drive in Jamaica; it's always insane. Have you ever seen the bumper stickers that say, "If You Don't Like My Driving – Stay Off the Sidewalks"? Well, that saying speaks of how the majority of Jamaicans drive in the 25-mile-wide country. I usually have my eyes closed and scream at the top of my lungs the entire time he's driving. *Sounds relaxing, doesn't it?*

During the whole drive along the gorgeous coastline, I couldn't believe how much litter was alongside the road and the coast. It was horrible. I then thought of creating a holiday we'll call *Beautify Jamaica Mon Day*. *Get it? It will be on a Monday.* (I told you that this will be a Nobel Peace Prize contender, didn't I?) I would have it twice a year —on Martin Luther King's and Bob Marley's birthdays. Everyone in a household 10 years old and older would get $50 a day to clean up the country and coastline. They would work from 8:00 a.m. to 6:00 p.m. with an hour break to eat jerk chicken (provided by the largest local Jamaican jerk chicken restaurant). The money would come from the government, the all-inclusive resorts, and the Jamaican Visitors Bureau. The discretionary income of each family would go up by approximately $800 annually. Not only would everyone have a way to make money that they didn't have before, but the country can be easily cleaned up in a 2-day period, when they have everyone working hard for 9 hours. So, that's my idea for Jamaica (it could probably work for any other tourism-driven country).

OK, now let's get back to America for my second idea. Also, please note that I actually wrote this chapter a year ago, and I believe that President Obama basically talks about my idea with a few changes. Hmm, I wonder if he overheard me rambling to Sven somewhere? That's all right, I don't really care who gets the credit for it, as long as it is done quickly!

I hate the fact that here in the U.S., our children are so under-educated compared to other countries. It's amazing and so unjust. Lately, you hear about how many kids can't afford to go even to a 2-year college because of the escalating costs. So here comes idea #2.

How about if we tax a set amount from every damn corporation a set amount that has fired their American workforce and gone abroad to India, China, the Philippines, etc., to get much cheaper labor. We will tax the corporation on each employee that they fired and then allocate the money to a paid Associates Degree for an American student. If the student wants to pursue a 4-year degree, the costs will be greatly subsidized by these companies. Think what will happen! The colleges will have more income; the teachers will make more, owing to supply and demand; costs will go down for families; discretionary incomes will go up, and that money can be used for consumer spending; there will be a much larger demand for teachers, and that will lead to higher salaries for teachers. College towns will thrive because of the abundance of students who have more discretionary dollars to spend. More students mean more restaurants, bookstores, computer stores, rental property, supermarkets, health care facilities, etc. Then *voila!* We will now have a country of better-educated youth who are ready to fill the positions that have now been created from all the new demand!

See what happens when poor Sven is stuck in the car with me for seven hours? Yes, I know that this is a lot to think about, and definitely my ideas have some huge kinks that need to be worked out in order for everything to go smoothly. But, what do you think, BFFs? Laura Ray has a dream and she's sticking to it! Who knows, if these dreams ever do come true, I wouldn't even care if I am passed over by the Nobel committee.

A Jamaican delicacy that is phenomenal even if you're not sitting at Bob Marley's favorite beach!

-

BROTHER DAVID'S TO-DIE-FOR JAMAICAN RED SNAPPER

2 to 3 pounds red snapper
2 large onions, chopped
2 medium–size carrots, thinly sliced
1 red pepper, seeded and cut into thin strips
1 yellow pepper, seeded and cut into thin strips
2 cloves garlic, finely minced
2 tbsp peanut or corn oil
1 bay leaf
1 tsp dried thyme
2 tsp allspice berries (optional)
1/2 tsp crushed red pepper
2 to 4 tsp salt
2 to 4 tsp black pepper
¾ to 1 cup malt vinegar
1/4 cup water
3 limes or lemons, sliced into wedges
1/2 teaspoon salt
1/3 cup flour
1/2 cup peanut or corn oil
2 Tbsp lemon or lime juice

In a large stainless steel saucepan, add all the vegetables, garlic, bay leaf, thyme, allspice, crushed pepper, and salt and pepper. Stir under medium-low heat for about 5 minutes.
Add vinegar, water, and lemon juice. Stir.
Cover the pan and simmer for 15 minutes, stirring occasionally, until vegetables are tender.
Wash the red snapper thoroughly in water with lemon or lime juice. Dry fish thoroughly.
Mix the salt and pepper and coat the fish.
Pour the flour into a plastic or brown paper bag.
Add the fish to the bag and shake until the fish is covered with flour.
Heat the oil in a large stainless steel skillet (Don't use a cast iron skillet!

Vinegar won't interact with the cast iron.)
Fry the fish until golden brown (3 - 4 minutes on each side)
Remove the fish to a large platter and spoon the hot vegetables and sauce over the fish.
Top with lime wedges and serve immediately.

Chapter 24

And Sometimes It Just Becomes Absurd

Let me begin this chapter by saying that we all try to be the best Moms (and Dads, of course, if any men are reading this) that we possibly can be. It's not rocket science to realize that the median age for first-time parents has gone way up since our parents had us. By the time I had Maggie and Mollie, I was in my late 30s and was actually one of the youngest women in my Lamaze class. It's crazy to think that my mother had all four of her children by the time she was 25 years old. She was just a kid. I, on the other hand was pretty darn close to getting my AARP card at the same time I was beginning to learn how to "Hoo Hoo Hee." How did Billy Crystal say it in *When Harry Met Sally?* (*One of my all-time favorite movies.*) I think he said something like, "You can *make them*; you just can't *pick them up* anymore."

I guess it's a good thing that parents are "older and wiser" now when they begin to have a family. The upside is that most of us should have higher discretionary incomes, live in better homes, and —most important — have the ability to spend more time with our children than our parents did. But, the downside is that because we have higher discretionary incomes and live in better homes, we have more time to spend with our children and spoil them rotten. Did you hear that there is now a name for us? They call us Helicopter Moms — parents who just spend their lives hovering over their children.

There is not a club, private school, sporting event, camp in the Far East, or "Become a Broadway Star" camp in the Catskills that is too much for our children. We want to do everything humanly possible to make sure that all our children have the most loving, wonderful, exciting childhoods that anyone could imagine.

I look back now and think, you know, my sisters, brother, Sven and I (and for that matter, 92 percent of all the people I knew growing up) didn't turn out so bad, even with parents who would rather go golfing or bowling; or play bridge and drink Scotch; or, in Sven's case, parents who would rather be hunting, fishing, or going to church. We all had jobs by the time we were 13, whether or not it was legal; or we'd be babysitting, mowing lawns, or working at the local DQ, dipping Dilly Bars for a whopping $1.15/hour in order to have enough money to buy our own clothes (*because our parents would buy us two pairs of jeans, one pair of shoes, and a few tops for the entire school year*), or to have any kind of spending money. (In Sven's case, his money was for buying James Brown and Rolling Stone albums that he had to sneak into his parents' house and play quietly after everyone had gone to sleep). Our parents expected us to play outside until about a half-hour after it became dark, and if we were thirsty, there were always hoses outside!

Don't you think that that it's gotten insane lately, with our kids and their iPhones, iPods, iPads, and $150 UGG boots. I won't generalize; I'll just say that our kids don't want for a damn thing and the entitlement quotient I'm seeing is enough for me to begin the "UGGly cry."

This brings me to my little story, which really made me stop in my "helicopter" tracks and made me realize how absurd we have all become. A few years back, Mollie was invited to one of her best friends' birthday party. Mollie's friend is an only child, and her parents have always gone way over the Chuck E. Cheese birthday party standard, which had always been a mainstay in our home. Heck, the parties were only three hours out of your life; all the coupons they sent made it a real bargain; and your home stayed intact. Best of all, you didn't have to have to endure 23 of your daughter's closest friends spending the night, with at least three puking at 3 a.m. from too much sugar. I finally stopped the family tradition once the kids reached fourteen. I had a feeling that they might just get a little peer backlash if I extended it any longer.

Mollie's best friend's mom has a much bigger imagination than I, and basically has a lot more free time than *moi* as well. When we got the golden invitation, professionally calligraphied, I thought, "God, this kid is turning seven. I can't wait to see what happens when she turns Sweet Sixteen!"

The theme of the party was the Academy Awards, and each of the girls was to dress up like their favorite award-winning actress. Hmm, the only actresses my kid was aware of were Cinderella, Jasmine, and the Little Mermaid. It kind of reminded me of that crazy and very dry comedian Steven Wright. He would do a joke that was kind of like, "I love the Stones. Fred and Wilma just crack me up, and that Barney Rubble, what an actor!"

OK, so I'm rambling again. The point was, this party was going to be *big* in Suburbiaville. The *Suburban Journal* was even doing a story on it (*must have been a very slow news day*). The mom and dad spent weeks planning. They got a long red carpet and ordered little naked man statues to give out. There were a ton of other details (*which I've repressed*) to encompass the whole Hollywood razzle dazzle. God forbid our kid didn't look presentable as her favorite actress.

Sven and I racked our brains to figure out who the heck Mollie could dress up as, when she walked into the kitchen telling us that she decided to be Shirley Temple. I had totally forgotten that when she was sick with that dreadful swine flu, I had ordered all my favorite Shirley Temple movies online. They really are adorable, even though they are about seventy years old (but who's counting?), and Mollie had actually become obsessed watching them. Heck, it could be much worse, don't you think? *Especially now, in the land of Teen Mom and Honey Boo Boo!*

So, the wholesome decision had been made. I was relieved and worried at the same time. We were now in the 3rd millennium and Shirley Temple is now about 108, (*looking fine, I may say*), but I knew that finding an Academy-Award-winning outfit for my 6-year-old would not be an easy feat.

No worries. There were several great costume places downtown (even though this was in the spring and Halloween was nowhere close). So, I began by using my handy dandy Yellow pages and called all the costume stores that I knew of, and no one had anything in stock that could even resemble dear Shirley.

I remembered that my sister Babs had bought her daughter an adorable blue satin dress years ago from a very la-de-da boutique. We were thrilled and amazed that it fit Mollie. Now, all we had to do was to find shoes (no big deal) and a wig. Mollie and I went to about four different wig and costume stores, and at our last one, we finally found the perfect wig that fit her little head.

We were both so giddy with excitement that the outfit was put together that we stopped at Icky Mickie's (my name for that restaurant with the golden arches) to use their bathroom to change in. Then we drove home. I called Maggie and Sven to tell them that an Academy-Award-winning actress was arriving home in minutes.

Sven and Maggie were waiting in the driveway for us when I pulled in. Mollie excitedly jumped out of her car seat and started to dance around. Sven very solemnly looked at her and whispered in my ear,

"Oh Hon, I'm not sure if she looks like Shirley Temple or the love child of Harpo Marx."

Even though he totally killed the moment for me, once again my man nailed it. (Look at the photo on the last page of the recipe photos and see if you agree with him.)

I tried to find one of my favorite recipes that matched her wig. Isn't that what all Helicopter Moms do?

SHIRLEY'S DELICIOUS SWIRLEY NOODLES MACARONI & CHEESE

1 1/2 cups uncooked elbow macaroni
2 tbsp butter
2 tbsp all-purpose flour
1/4 cup milk
1 cup half-and-half
1/4 tsp paprika
1/2 tsp pepper
2-1/2 cups shredded cheddar cheese, divided
salt to taste
1 cup soft bread crumbs, tossed with 1-1/2 tablespoons melted butter

Preheat oven to 350 degrees

Cook noodles in boiling salted water according to package directions; drain well and set aside.
Meanwhile, melt butter in a medium saucepan over low heat. Blend in flour, stirring constantly, until smooth and bubbly. Gradually stir in milk and half-and-half. Cook, stirring constantly, until mixture boils and thickens, about 2 to 3 minutes. Remove from heat and add paprika, pepper, and 2 cups of the cheese. Stir until cheese is melted and sauce is smooth.
Combine sauce with the macaroni and add salt to taste.
Spoon into a buttered 1-1/2-quart casserole dish. Garnish top with remaining 1/2 cup of cheese and dot with additional butter.
Last step, scatter the buttered bread crumbs evenly over the cheese.
Bake for 25 to 30 minutes, until lightly browned and bubbly.

Hope you enjoy!

Chapter 25

A Simple Way To Piss Off A Total Stranger

So, you know how we, as Women of the Millennium, run ourselves ragged every day of the year trying to please our husbands, our children (who have gotten used to us being at their beck and call 24/7) and our bosses – who expect us to do bigger and better things year after year after year after year. And you know how things just simply multiply to absolutely stupid proportions around the holidays…well that is the subject of today's chapter.

No, I promise, I won't complain about being under-appreciated and proceed to have my own little pity party… you, my new Best Friend will say, "Been there/Done that, Laura."

I promise, I won't be the Laura Ray martyr any longer. But, I couldn't tell you what happened today and have you understand how easily it could happen to you as well, without prefacing the above.

After working all day, trying to meet my quota — which, by the way, always happens to be twice as big in December — I never understand the logic. Especially because the last thing people want to talk about right before the holidays is "work" and how to spend money on not-so-fun stuff, but it just has always been that way; and of course the corporate hierarchy above me has never asked me for my opinion. Go figure?!?

I had to go to Mollie's 6 p.m. Christmas/Chanukah choir performance. Digressing yet again, I think there are two damn, over-done Chanukah songs ever written versus the 12,245 beautiful melodic Christmas tunes.

But, in order to be politically correct, those who make all of the public school musical choice decisions feel like they have to throw them into the mix every time just to make sure that "we Jews" don't feel totally left out. I'm going to go out on the proverbial limb on this one and bet if someone out there were to take a survey to see if we would prefer to never ever have to hear "Dreidel Dreidel Dreidel, I Made You Out of Clay" again in our lifetime, it would be a resounding "Thank you, God!"

After the performance, I then had a whopping six minutes to change from my drab work clothes to something a little more festive and wrap some presents for a girlfriend holiday get-together that we all had to reschedule about nine times to finally find a time that all of us could make. Then order a pizza and chicken fingers for the kids (you just have to have a little protein in the nutritional dinner, don't you think?) and in the meantime, I had to get the loaf of bread out of the oven and the Matzoh Ball/chicken soup off the stove that I made during my lunch hour for my co-worker and friend, Ethel (the namesake of those fabulous "Oreo Balls" from my last book, remember?) who had a terrible case of the flu.

Loading up my car with the gifts, the cookie trays that I made for all of my girlfriends the night before, and the chicken soup and bread for Ethel, my car looked as though I was ready for a sojourn across the country. It smelled absolutely wonderful with the soup, the bread and the eighteen types of cookies, but it was so packed that I couldn't see out the window.

Just like clockwork, to make my day perfect, it started to sleet. I called Ethel from my cell phone to make sure that she was at her home so that I could quickly drop off the meal for her family. She didn't answer her phone, so I called her cell phone, and she didn't answer that one either. I thought, "Oh, that's great! Now, I have about eight gallons of very hot matzoh ball soup spilling all over the backseat of my car, and she's not home.

I decided to give it one last-ditch effort, and called her again. Heck, I was already thirty minutes late to my party; and finally someone answered the phone. I said, with a huge sigh of relief, "Oh, Thank Goodness You're Home!" I continued with, "I'm late, so I'll have to hurry up and run the soup into your house, so please have the door unlocked for me." She said, "Oh, You shouldn't have, that is so sweet of you. What time do you think you'll get here?"

I said, "Probably in about ten minutes." She then said, "Perfect! Thank you so much. You really shouldn't have gone through so much trouble for 'little old me.'"

She continued, "I've felt so bad all day long, this will be just what the doctor ordered!"

I continued with, "Well, what did the doctor say?"

"He said that I need to take a Z-Pack and hopefully in five days it will do the trick, but right now, I'm feeling totally miserable," she said.

I tried to make her feel better by replying, "I'm so sorry, and really, it's no big deal at all… in fact, if I do say so myself, it looks like one of the best batches of matzoh ball soup I've ever made, and you know what everyone calls it, Jewish Penicillin!!!!"

She said, "I've actually never had matzoh ball soup before and I can't wait to try it."

I paused for a few seconds while at the same time, dodging huge sleet balls on my windshield, and said, "You've got to be kidding, of course you've had matzoh ball soup, in fact, I think I like your soup recipe better than my own!" She said, "No really, I've never tried it before in my life!"

I then paused again and said, "Who is this? Isn't this Ethel?"

She then very politely said, "No, it's Darlene."

I suddenly just cracked up realizing that I had just had a very meaningful conversation with a total stranger. I then looked at the phone I was talking into and saw that I had transposed the last two numbers. As I was giggling like an absolute idiot, while at the same time, feeling like a total schmuck, I said, "Oh Darlene, I'm so sorry, I meant to dial 570-0225 instead of 570-0252."

She didn't say anything for a while (it seemed like five minutes) and then very somberly said, "Well, does that mean I'm not getting any soup?"

(Quick little sidenote: To those of you who know my grave affliction with G.T.; if I hadn't been so late for my dinner party and afraid that I was going to miss out on all of the good sushi, I would have just found out where she lived and split the pot with her).

In my humble opinion, The second best Matzoh Ball Soup Recipe

MATZOH BALL SOUP WITH EGG NOODLES, TOO!
(Not intended for Passover, of course!!!)

CHICKEN SOUP:
6 boneless uncooked chicken breasts sliced in nice size pieces
4 large celery stalks cut up in medium size pieces
1 small bag of small, pre-cleaned carrots
1 large onion sliced in medium size pieces
3 tablespoons of parsley
3 chicken soup bullion cubes
2 cans of 14oz. chicken broth (no MSG)
salt & pepper to taste
1 large bag of frozen Reames Homestyle Egg Noodles (you find them in the frozen food department by the frozen pasta)

MATZOH BALLS:
4 eggs divided
4 tbsp. chicken soup broth
1 cup of matzoh meal
2 tsp. of salt
¼ cup hot water

In the largest soup pot that you have, fill ½ with water and then add the first 8 ingredients (everything but the noodles) to the pot.
Let it cook until it starts to boil, and then add the egg noodles.
Bring the heat down to a simmer and cover.
In a mixing bowl, beat the 4 egg whites until they peak. Gently fold in the salt, 4 beaten egg yolks, matzoh meal, and hot water. Lightly stir and cover the mixture. Refrigerate for one hour.
Bring soup to a slow boil again and form matzoh ball mixture into balls the size of walnuts. Carefully drop the matzoh balls into the soup so that they don't touch each other. Cover the pot and cook for another 20 minutes. Serve large helpings in large bowls with crackers and crusty bread.
Enjoy!

Chapter 26

I Continually Tell Myself How Truly Blessed I am

It's so bizarre how the human mind works — or should I say the strange mind of Laura Ray. I've been extremely happily married to Sven for 8 years now. Very little drama and a ton of love. What a concept! I always say that I absolutely love marriage, I just hated my first (*and second*) husband.

I don't know about you, but as a single woman, I was an absolutely horrible dater. I hated every minute of it, even though I knew that it was a necessary evil to date a man before I fell in love with him and then be happily married to him. I guess I wouldn't have had to date all those "frogs" if I was one of those 6th-century Jewish or Chinese women who were never given a choice. And honestly, who am I kidding? Who could have made a worse choice for a husband than I did choosing P.D.? But, digressing once again, because I was determined to find the true love of my life (*who I knew was out there somewhere*) and to show Maggie and Mollie what a loving relationship should be like, and because I was a modern woman of the millennium (*whatever the heck that is*), I knew that I would have to put myself out there to find Mr. Right.

I've also decided that as long as my new best friends are asking me, my books are going to be an every-other-year occurrence. Because: #1 – Unfortunately, I know that things will continue to happen to me that you will all relate to; and #2 – I've had such great responses about all the recipes I've shared with you. I really think that if I can help even a little bit with making your lives a little easier, then Laura Ray has accomplished one thing to help women-kind.

So, this is just my way of telling you that once again I'm going to end the second installment of "Brain Dead in the Burbs" with a story of one of my most horrible dates. It actually was so damn horrible, that I had repressed it and hadn't even told Sven about it until yesterday.

It's funny (*in a twisted and sad kind of way*) that when I speak to women's groups, it's this chapter that women bring up a lot. It's like a sad competition that begins with, "Oh, my God, I think I dated that horrible psychiatrist that you dated. Was his name Vernon?" Or, "If you think you had bad luck with men, let me tell you what happened to me last week!"

Before I tell you my last wretched dating story for this year, please let me thank you for being the best sounding board I've ever had. I truly appreciate your friendship and understanding, and I'm looking forward to seeing you at a book club or bookstore in the very near future!

OK, here it goes. A long, long time ago, one of my best friends told me that her cousin's cousin by marriage was a really nice guy who was a realtor who had 2 children, and she always thought that he and I would get along perfectly. Swearing off all "friends of friends" or "cousins of cousin's friends" I found it ironic and hopefully a *cosmic sign* that, a few days later, I found this same guy on the Jewish dating service that my friend (*who insisted that I start to date Jewish guys*) subscribed me to.

Very maturely, I made the first move and contacted him and told him that I had heard wonderful things about him. We e-mailed back and forth a few times before we decided to take the old "*one date cannot kill you*" plunge.

He sounded sweet, but the only thing he seemed to want to talk about was his lovely home in "Blackerby Estates." It was a bit alarming to me that he didn't really want to talk about his children, his family, his pets, his job, his political affiliations, his hobbies, the last book he read, etc. He really only wanted to talk about the big house he owned.

I must admit, I've never been a real estate elitist, nor have I ever been invited to join la-de-da country clubs (you are totally shocked, aren't you?). I've never set my sights very high with houses. I remember how excited I was when I bought my first house and it had a laundry chute! (*I knew that I had hit the big time!*) So, it didn't really shock me that in all my years on this planet, I had never heard about this seemingly well-to-do area in our city. Nor could I really care less that he lived in a mansion.

Anyway, when he insisted on starting our first date at his house, I just assumed (*correctly, it turned out*) that he wanted to show it off to me. He said, "Why don't you come here and I can show you my house, and then we can walk to this quaint restaurant near Blackerby Estates. (*He had to get in the name of his subdivision just one more time, just in case I had forgotten it after the 297th mention.*)

Not having been on a date for quite some time, I was fine with it. I had already had a strong intuition that he wasn't going to be my "Sven," but what the heck, I may just be horribly wrong with my intuition, or he may end up becoming a good friend, or maybe just know someone who is more compatible with me.

When I walked into his home, I immediately started to sweat through my new outfit. I couldn't believe it! I had just bought this really cute silk summer dress and I was ruining it within the first 20 minutes of wearing it! (*Don't you just hate when that happens? Plus, I'm really not someone who perspires in abundance.*)

He looked at my flushed face and said, "Oh, I'm sorry that you're so hot. I try to save money any way I can so that I can afford to live in this house." I realized that the air conditioner must have been set on 92 degrees, and that there was only one light on in the entire old mansion. Boy, he really was trying to save some money!

I tried to be as polite as I could possibly be, even though I was probably about three minutes away from having heat stroke and passing out right on his 17th-century terrazzo floor, and said, "That is all right, Ned. Let's just go outside and we can walk to the restaurant." (*I knew that even walking in the humid, hot St. Louis August weather would be more comfortable than sitting in his house.*)

We started to walk, and the doofus tried to hold my sweaty hand with his sweaty hand. I just pretended that I didn't notice and stepped about

1-1/2 steps away from him.

The silence was deafening, and we had an entire mile to go, so we just started talking about what middle-aged individuals talk about so well on a first date, and that would be about their divorces. He wanted me to go first. So, I told my entire Psycho Dick story as quickly as I could. I told him about my two wonderful daughters and my good job, and I threw in my small (*but very air conditioned*) home.

It was his turn. He looked at me and became very serious and spoke in a very low, sad voice. I quickly forgot about his snobby real estate or his Costa-Rican-jungle-atmosphere home and started to feel sorry for him.

He began with, "Well, Laura, I don't know if you know this or not, but I had kidney disease and almost died." (*Oh no….I felt tears welling up, but hoped he would just think it was sweat.*)

I said, "Oh, Ned, I'm so sorry. I had no idea! You look totally healthy now. Congratulations!" He continued, "Well, I was in and out of hospitals for two years and almost died. Finally, a miracle happened, and after having no luck at all being on the kidney transplant recipient list, my wife got tested and they found that she was a perfect match for me!"

"Oh, my God, Ned! That's fantastic! How amazing is that?! What a fantastic gift to give to a spouse! She saved your life, didn't she?" And then I stopped and said, "So, I don't understand, what happened?"

He looked at me, and as God is my witness, he said, "Well, Laura, that is the strange part." He continued, "It's very difficult to explain, but when you're in a life-and-death situation like I was, your outlook on life completely changes. You begin to re-evaluate everything." He said, "I realized that I never really loved my wife, and now that I had a second chance in life, I needed to start over and find someone who can really make me happy!"

I don't know what came over me, but I just stopped dead in the middle of the street and said (which I'm really not proud of), in a pretty loud, obnoxious voice, "*God, I hate when that happens!*" He looked at me, bewildered, and said, "What are you talking about, Laura?"

I just looked at him, still not moving and said, "*Well, you know — when you give someone a major organ and then they realize they really don't love you!"*

I think he was totally speechless, because we just looked at each other and didn't say one more word. We turned around and walked back to his very warm mansion so that I could get into my air conditioned car and leave.

For this chapter, even though I thought it would be cute to have a great chili recipe with many types of "kidney" beans, I think it would be more apropos to have another cocktail recipe. (*This will be another tradition for my book. After every dating chapter will come a much-needed recipe containing alcohol.*)

This is one of my favorite drinks ever. It's delicious, refreshing, fun to serve, and quickly does "the trick." I hope you love it as much as I do.

KATHY'S DRUNKO BUNKO SLUSHO

2 cups of sugar
6 oz. can of frozen lemonade concentrate
6 oz. can of orange juice concentrate
4 cups ice tea
3 cups Bourbon (Kathy likes Canadian Mist)
7-Up

In large bowl, mix all liquid and sugar together until sugar has been completely dissolved.

Cover and freeze overnight.

When you serve, scoop out ½ of slush in cocktail glass and ½ 7-Up. Enjoy and 'Say Goodnight'!

About the Author

Laura Roodman Edwards Ray lives in a suburb of St. Louis, Missouri with her two daughters, her loving husband, and a stepson close by. She is a full-time mom, law firm sales representative, co-producer/co-director of Listen to Your Mother - St. Louis, speaker, and author. She is currently finishing the third volume of her twisted trilogy called "Forever Brain Dead" and plans on making it an annual occurrence if anyone would like to continue reading the strange stories of her life and pick up great recipes at the same time.

She still welcomes anyone from the "Smoking Gun" or any other "truthful literary agency" to try to prove that her memoirs are made up at all. That would be a lot less embarrassing to her, as well as to her family.